£4·50
US $8.95
CAN $10.95

CONTENTS

DOCTOR WHO YEARBOOK ™ is published annually by Marvel Comics Ltd., 13/15 Arundel Street, London WC2R 3DX, Tel: 071-497 2121. All *Doctor Who* material is © 1992 BBC. Daleks © 1992 Terry Nation. All Brief Encounters © their respective authors. Future Dalek design © Raymond P Cusick. All other material is © Marvel Comics Ltd., unless otherwise stated. **The Doctor Who Yearbook 1993** was created by Gary Russell and Peri Godbold, with John Freeman, Chris McCormack, Fiona Moscatelli, Ed Lawrance, Stuart Bartlett and not forgetting Louise Cassell. Advisor: John Nathan-Turner. Editorial Director: Paul Neary. Managing Director: Vincent Conran. Front cover: Dalek photograph © Steve Cook - various Doctor photographs © BBC. No similarity between any of the fictional names, characters, persons and/or institutions herein with those of any living or dead persons or institutions is intended and any such similarity which may exist is purely coincidental. Nothing may be reproduced by any means in whole or part without the written permission of the publishers. **The Doctor Who Yearbook 1993** is an associate publication of **Doctor Who Magazine**, published every four weeks. Subscription and back issue information from: **Doctor Who Magazine**, PO Box 500, Leicester, Great Britain, LE99 0AB. "If you ever wondered how I got to be Emperor of the Daleks, this Yearbook's got all the answers!" declared Davros happily munching on another Thal-pate sandwich. Printed in Italy.

SPEARHEADS FROM SPACE

"In the last decade we've been sending probes deeper and deeper into space. We've paid attention to ourselves..." Certainly the planet Earth seems to be among the most vulnerable to alien invasion – and also to invasions with their origins closer to home...

The first alien invasion of Earth to be featured in *Doctor Who* was *The Dalek Invasion of Earth*, screened in 1964 and set about a hundred years later. The Daleks were already in control, having invaded in 2157. They bombarded the planet with meteorites and plague – then when they landed there was little resistance. By the time the first Doctor and his companions arrived it was all over.

Of course the Doctor defeated the Daleks and the plan to turn the Earth into a giant spaceship. Not that the Daleks were that easily defeated. They managed to change the course of history so that they invaded in an alternate future, after a world war was sparked off by the destruction of the peace conference at Auderley House. When the Third Doctor and Jo are plunged into the twenty-second century in *Day of the Daleks* (shown in 1972), the invasion is again a *fait accompli* – with the Daleks this time supported by the Ogrons and human traitors rather than the brainwashed Robomen of their 'first' attempt.

But the *fait accompli* is the exception in *Doctor Who*. Usually the Doctor is in at the start of events. In *The Android Invasion* (1975), it seems as if the Doctor and Sarah have arrived when the invasion is already in full swing – a bridgehead established by the Kraals and their android doubles of the local population. But in fact this is just a training exercise – the invasion is yet to start, and the Doctor and Sarah are able to reach Earth with the spearhead and warn the authorities. (That story also seems to show the death of the popular RSM Benton, when his android double ordered the removal of his body – but fear not. The Brigadier tells the Doctor he's alive and well in the 1983 story, *Mawdryn Undead*.)

ESTABLISHING BRIDGEHEADS

One of the best known attempted invasions, foiled by the Doctor in mid-stride, is the Nestenes' *Spearhead from Space* – the first challenge to the Doctor's third incarnation in 1970. Best remembered for the scenes of the Auton dummies smashing their way out of shop windows, the Doctor is able to defeat the Nestenes with the help of UNIT as he takes up his post as their scientific adviser.

Like the Daleks, the Nestenes are not to be put off easily. In the following season (shown in 1971) they were back, helped by the Master in his first story – *Terror of the Autons*. This time their invasion was to follow the confusion and terror caused by the deaths inflicted by deadly plastic daffodils. The Doctor again averted disaster.

In *The Invasion* (1968), the Cybermen used a similar technique of immobilising the population. But they did it through paralysis induced by a signal generated by the micro-monolithic circuit, built into almost all electronic equipment by International Electromatics and its boss Tobias Vaughn. Vaughn was under Cyber control, but repented enough to help the Doctor and UNIT destroy the invading Cybermen troops, while Zoe and the army took care of the invasion fleet with missiles.

Most clandestine of all was the invasion attempted by Axos – a living spaceship in *The Claws of Axos* (1971). Far from trying to hide or sneak onto the planet, Axos arrived to offer the Earth a marvellous gift – Axonite. But Axonite was not the wonderful substance it seemed, able to enlarge and copy living material. It was actually all part of the Axos creature – which was about to feed on the planet Earth and drain it of all energy, through the Axonite distributed about the Earth. Again the Doctor was able to defeat the menace, with the help of the allegiance-switching Master. ►

Visitors from Axos. Photo © BBC Video

Photo © BBC

5

In *Four to Doomsday*, Monarch (Stratford Johns) prepared to enslave Earth through his cybernetic humans. The Master (Roger Delgado) has been responsible for bringing many alien invaders to Earth, incuding the Autons and the Axons. The Cybermen hid in the London sewers during two attempts to rule the Earth, firstly in *The Invasion* and again in *Attack of the Cybermen*. All photos © BBC

Some invasions were already in progress by the time the Doctor stumbled upon them. If it can be described as an invasion attempt, then this is the status of the Great Intelligence's grand plan when the Doctor encounters *The Abominable Snowmen* in Tibet in the 1920s (broadcast in 1967). And years later he meets not just Colonel Lethbridge-Stewart but also Yeti in the London Undergound in *The Web of Fear* (1968) with the Great Intelligence's second screened invasion well underway.

Similarly the Ice Warriors have already taken over the Moon when the Doctor gets involved in *The Seeds of Death* (1969) and are about to unleash deadly Martian fungus on the Earth. The Cybermen too get a stage further (as we saw in 1982). In their plan to invade Earth to destroy an anti-Cyber conference they have already planted their *Earthshock* bomb and the troops to follow up and kill any survivors are in transit on the freighter.

In *The Masque of Mandragora* it is the Doctor himself who transports the invader – a portion of the Mandragora Helix – to Earth, where it possesses first the astrologer Hieronymous, then the brethren of the cult of Demnos. It plans to take over Earth before Man can learn from the discoveries of the Renaissance, and it will start by wiping out Leonardo and the other great Italian thinkers.

FULL-FRONTAL ATTACKS

How Monarch, in *Four To Doomsday* (1982) intends to conquer the Earth is never made clear – and the Doctor defeats him before he arrives on the planet, the culmination of many earlier visits. Perhaps he is planning the sort of head-on attack that the Cybermen launch in 1986 on the Snowcap Base in *The Tenth Planet*, the first Doctor's final battle shown in 1966. Their invasion of the base is a one of necessity to them – they have to destroy the Earth before Mondas absorbs too much energy from it and explodes. They make another attempt to avert the destruction of their first home world in *Attack of the Cybermen* (1985), hiding in the sewers again after *The Invasion*.

In *Silver Nemesis* (1988) we must assume that the Cybermen are planning to invade Earth in force, although the main action centres on their desire to possess the statue of Lady Peinforte made from the powerful living metal, Validium – which the Doctor uses to destroy their fleet. Certainly invasion is their purpose when they take over *The Moonbase* (1967) and its weather control machine the Gravitron. But on this occasion too the Doctor was able to turn their own weapon against them – using the gravity field of the

Gravitron to shoot the Cybermen and their equipment off into far space.

Another Cyber attempt to invade the Earth got no further than their preparatory take-over of *The Wheel in Space* which they intended to use as a staging post for their attack (screened in 1968). This time they were assisted by the Cybermats, and the Cybermen themselves were seen to hatch from giant eggs on the spaceship *Silver Carrier*.

However, for sheer brute force, the Daleks take the biscuit. True in *The Daleks' Master Plan* (1965/66) they have enlisted the services of the treacherous Guardian of the Solar System, Mavic Chen, and built a powerful weapon – the Time Destructor – but they still aim to crush their enemies largely by force of arms. Likewise, in *Planet of the Daleks* (1973) they are happy for the Master and the Ogrons to prepare the way for invasion by setting off a conflict between Earth and Draconia (in the previous story, *Frontier in Space*). But they have a force of ten thousand Daleks concealed on Spiridon and learning the secret of invisibility, ready to follow through the attack.

Although the Daleks consciously plan to invade and conquer the Earth, others do it out of instinct or programming. The Krynoid takes over humans and animals as food – to survive – in *The Seeds of Doom* (1976).

Daleks conquer and destroy in *The Daleks' Master Plan*. Photo © Julian Vince. Plant life has proven to be a threat on more than one occasion. The Vervoids from *The Trial of a Time Lord*, and the Krynoid from *The Seeds of Doom*. Photos © BBC

Similarly, the Vervoids act out of an instinctive desire to survive, building the bodies of the humans they have killed into a huge compost heap (*Terror of the Vervoids* – 1986). The Malus war machine in *The Awakening* (1984) is programmed to take over the world using psychic energy, and to destroy itself if and when it fails.

INVADING TO SURVIVE

Less a matter of instinct, more of survival, is the attempted invasion of *The Ice Warriors* (1967) led by Vaarga. They believed their home planet (Mars) to be dead and uninhabitable, and so want to colonise the Earth. There are only a few survivors, but they distrust the humans – believing the ioniser used to stop the advancing glaciers of the next ice age is a weapon. Perhaps their fears are not so ill-founded, since they are destroyed by the humans using the ioniser on full power – a setting on which it can melt even rock.

The Zygons (*Terror of the Zygons*, 1975) find themselves in a similar situation. While they have been stranded on the bed on Loch Ness in their crippled spaceship, their home planet has been destroyed by solar flares. Now the survivors are on their way to Earth – at Zygon leader Broton's invitation. Until they arrive in several hundred years' time, Broton and his half-dozen colleagues aim to use human slaves to modify the planet so it is suitable for the Zygons. Amongst other things, he plans to destroy the polar ice caps – which Vaarga and his fellow warriors would no doubt have wanted to proliferate.

The small force of Terileptils who try to wipe out humanity with modified bubonic plague in *The Visitation* (1982), wish to do so mainly to save themselves the trouble of trying to coexist when they take over. Their invasion never really happens.

Two other invasions failed to take place; the Rutan one because the scouting team is destroyed and hence the Earth deemed too hazardous – *Horror of Fang Rock* (1977) – and the other, as revealed in *The Sontaran Experiment* (1975), because the surveyors are tricked into believing that an invasion is doomed to be thwarted by superior and informed forces.

In *The Mind Robber* (1968) the Master of Fiction says that the Earth is to be brought under control, but the Doctor destroys the controlling computer and fictional world before the invasion gets any further than this throwaway suggestion.

HOME-GROWN INVASIONS

Not all invasions are attempted by off-world aliens; some are home grown. The BOSS computer aims to take

Above: Harry Sullivan (Ian Marter) watches Broton (John Woodnutt) prepare his gambit in *Terror of the Zygons*. Photo © BBC Video. Middle: The Doctor (Peter Davison) and Jane Hampden (Polly James) try to avoid the Malus in *The Awakening*. Below: The Terileptils plan their tactics in *The Visitation*. Photos © BBC

Would-be inheritors of their planet, the Silurians and Sea Devils team-up in *Warriors of the Deep*. Photo © BBC

that humanity only exists in its current form as a vehicle for the manifestation of the Fendahl. The invasion (similar to the experiment carried out by *The Dæmons*, shown in 1971) took place twelve million years ago – and was a complete success. Earth has already been invaded and left as a legacy by the Fendahl – and we are the beneficiaries. As the research scientist in *Fendahl*, Adam Colby says, "We are *all* aliens."

Justin Richards

over the world in *The Green Death* (1973), although it could be argued that this will be through mind control rather than invasion as such. But the giant maggots which emerge from the Llanfairfach coal mines, grown huge on the waste materials from Global Chemicals, certainly threaten to take over the planet.

Similar in intent to BOSS is WOTAN in *The War Machines* (1966), which attempts to control Earth, or at least Britain, from the Post Office (now Telecom) Tower using its War Machines. Again this is to be a mental invasion.

But the Silurians (or Eocenes, as the Doctor renames them) and Sea Devils are determined to rid the Earth of its humans and retake the planet for themselves since they regard themselves as the superior race, having once ruled it about sixty-five million years ago. They attack from their Derbyshire caves in *Doctor Who and the Silurians* (1970), and the Brigadier blows them up. When they attack again, from underwater, in *The Sea Devils* (1972), the Doctor blows them up. And when Silurians and Sea Devils join forces in *Warriors of the Deep* (1984) – to try to start a war in which the humans will blow themselves up – the Doctor again thwarts them, despite his sympathy for their position.

Invasions of a sort are also attempted by the seaweed parasite monster in *Fury from the Deep* (1968), and as a means of clearing London for the time experiments of Professor Whitaker in *Invasion of the Dinosaurs* (1974).

Another story which could be classed as an invasion story is odd in that it has no aliens coming to Earth, or even creatures from Earth's past (or present) trying to take over. *Image of the Fendahl* (1977) suggests

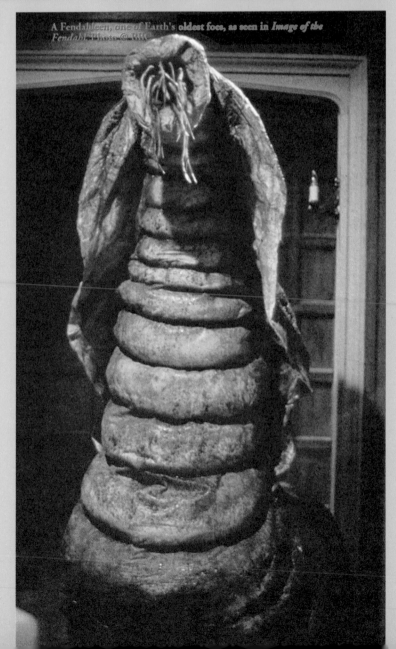

A Fendahleen, one of Earth's oldest foes, as seen in *Image of the Fendahl*. Photo © BBC

Cambridge Previsited

Buddy Holly was on the radio again. He could hear him caterwaulling, tinny and tuneless, out of the transistor radio of a passing third year. That was one of the few drawbacks to the planet on which he had chosen to spend his last few centuries — Earthlings had no sense of music.

He quickened his snail's pace and tried to focus his attention on getting to the College library. It wasn't easy. Earth was so different to Gallifrey – so green, so alive. None of the starched reservedness which walked the halls of the Capitol. Even the students here were a living hive of unpredictability and the love of life. When he spoke with them they were ever questioning, ever eager for knowledge. He found them all irritatingly fascinating.

It was such a pity that the entire planet was tone deaf.

He crossed the courtyard in a fairly respectable time, his willpower keeping his increasingly vague mind and mannerisms under tight control, and arrived at the doors to the library.

The audience of books greeted him as he entered. He was sure he had read almost every one of them in his time, and in times before that, and he fancied he could hear the characters of each novel talking to him as he passed.

None of the students looked up as he shuffled by, none smiled at him as he searched row after row of history. To them, he was just daft old Professor Chronotis. He had been at Cambridge forever and would still be there when they were in their graves. Nothing special.

Part of Chronotis' mind consi-

dered the huddled youngsters, bent determinedly over their assignments, unconsciously noting what each was doing and mentally correcting them when they erred. The youngsters were suddenly aware of the seemingly glaring errors they had made and corrected them accordingly, wondering why they couldn't shake the image of the old teacher mentally patting them on the head.

A hand touched Chronotis' shoulder and he jumped. Turning, he saw an elderly man in check trousers and an all consuming black cape. Pristine white cuffs peeked out from his sleeves and the Professor could just make out an immaculate cravat nestled at his throat. Time Lords have the ability to recognise their own kind, regardless of whichever body they happen to be in at the time, and Chronotis immediately sensed a colleague. No, more than that, they had met not so long ago. But what *was* the chap's name?

The old man sniffed disdainfully and his somewhat impatient eyes twinkled,

"My dear fellow, you're late. They said you never could keep track of time that well, could you hmm? Quite ironic for a Time Lord if you think about it."

Chronotis studied the man for a brief second and he frowned, "Your note was quite a surprise. 'Meet me in the library fifteen minutes ago' didn't exactly give me time to change and make myself presentable, did it?"

The old man laughed shortly. "You're a Time Lord, aren't you, eh? Yes, you should have used your skills. Or have all these years alone in one time and one place rotted your intellect?"

They eyed each other dangerously for the briefest of moments and then the old man held out his hand, "Professor Chronotis, I presume."

The Professor eyed the man warily, his head in a panic stricken whirl. If he guessed correctly, this was an earlier incarnation of the Doctor. He'd already met a tall, curly haired version, about four years back. Now, what was all that nonsense about causing irreparable rifts in the Time Lines? Oh, *why* hadn't he paid more attention? He smiled at the old man and chose the easy way out. "Have we met?"

"Not socially, no. But I have listened to the stories about you with interest."

Chronotis gasped, all surprise and

delight. He should have been an actor. "You're from Gallifrey!"

The old Doctor sighed impatiently, "Well, of course I am!"

"Oh, marvellous! My dear fellow it's good to see you, whoever you are."

They walked together for a while in the courtyard and talked of places past and times long gone. The Doctor marvelled at the Professor's choice of retirement in exile. "Being stranded in one time and place forever," he shook his head, "I could never stand it. No, I would go mad within a fortnight."

Chronotis suddenly developed a mild coughing fit and then shrugged, "I don't notice the time. There's so much to learn here, and so many people to meet that I never stop to get lonely." He smiled, "Besides, I find the students exhilarating – if a little frustratingly dense at times!" They were back in the library, now. He looked at the Doctor, "How's that young journalist, by the way?"

"Who?"

Chronotis bit his lip. Not an actor after all. A fool maybe. . .

"Sorry. No, nothing. Rambling a bit. It's my age, don't you know. Have you read *Treasure Island*? It's one of my favourites."

The Doctor watched Chronotis curiously. The poor old thing was obviously going senile. If he was ever able to return home he would put forward the idea that the retired Time Lord should be watched over. For his own safety, of course.

Chronotis was doddering along the aisle, enthusing over the stacks of books, "You haven't settled on Earth, have you?"

The Doctor shook his head sadly, "I did for a while in a few years time but I've had to move on since then. This visit is literally what you might call a flying one."

"Oh." Chronotis shuffled and looked at his feet, "I was rather hoping to have a like mind to talk to. But if you have to leave. . ." He didn't finish his sentence.

The Doctor reached up and took a book from one of the shelves. Dusting it off he handed it to Chronotis. "Here, read this and keep a copy close at hand all the time. You might find that it shows the potential of the human race a little clearer. They're not the backward race they have been taken for, you know."

The Professor looked at the book – *The Time Machine* by HG Wells. "Oh, yes, you mentioned that this was a good one." Oh no! What was he saying?

He looked up and was relieved to see the Doctor out of earshot, walking for the door. Replacing the book he raced after the Doctor with a surprising turn of speed. "Can't you stay for a while longer?" he pleaded, "There's so much we have to talk about."

"I'm afraid not. I get restless staying in one place for too long. I'm a traveller by nature, I'm afraid, and you could say that nature is calling."

Chronotis nodded, "Very well then. But promise me something?"

"What?"

"You will come and visit me again sometime, won't you?"

The Doctor smiled, "Without meaning to sound cliched, my friend, I'm afraid only time will tell!"

And he was gone.

Chronotis slumped against one of the bookshelves and let out his breath in a long sigh.

"Never again. Oh please, Rassilon, never again!" He needed some fresh air.

That night, while Chronotis was out buying some milk and sugar from a late-night shop, the stillness of his own quarters was disturbed. The Doctor's TARDIS materialised and into the gloom stepped the Doctor pleased his short trip through the vortex had been accurate. After his extremely strange afternoon with the Professor, he realised he never actually read *Treasure Island*.

Leaving his companions sleeping inside the Ship, he crept out, everlasting match in hand, intending to borrow a copy for the evening.

The flicker of light played across the countless shelves in Chronotis' study, stacked with books. Biographies, childrens' stories, science and nature books until finally – a small gathering of fiction.

After a few minutes search, he found *Treasure Island*, between a first edition *Peter Rabbit* and a small, thick brown spined old book.

Drawing *Treasure Island* out with his thin fingers, he reached up and slotted into its place a paperback copy of *The Time Machine*, as a replacement. "Fair exchange is not robbery, hmm?" he muttered, smiling.

A door outside Chronotis' rooms, at the end of the hallway, slammed. It might have been Chronotis returning, or just Wilkin, the Porter doing his late-night rounds. Regardless, the Doctor darted back into the TARDIS like a frightened rabbit and seconds later the Ship was gone.

Undisturbed, alongside its new neighbour, the thick brown book stood proudly on the shelf, ignored. Embossed, but faint with age, its title read: *The Ancient Law of Gallifrey. . .*

One day, someone would finally remove it. And try to read it. Until then, it sat there, patiently waiting. . .

Karen Dunn

Monster File
The ICE WARRIORS

The Monster of Peladon Photograph © BBC - Art © David Lloyd

NAME: The Ice Warriors

PLANET OF ORIGIN: Mars

KNOWN ALLIES: The Galactic Federation

KNOWN ENEMIES: (Originally) The Doctor; (Currently) Enemies of the Galactic Federation

BASE OF OPERATIONS: Mobile

FIRST APPEARANCE: *The Ice Warriors*

The term Ice Warriors was first coined by the human archaeologists who discovered a Martian spaceship buried beneath a glacier on Earth during the Ice Age of the Thirty-First century.

The Martians were a warrior species, dedicated to war during the earliest parts of their history. However, towards the end of the third millennia, the Martians gave up their militaristic ways, although their society was still ordered on a feudal structure. The Martians became leading members of The Galactic Federation and were instrumental in many diplomatic missions to welcome planets into the ever-growing alliance.

Fragmented factions of Martians still existed, however, always determined to restore the Martian race to their former war-like ways. These groups proved small in number and easily overpowered by the main Federation forces.

Monster File
The ZYGONS

Terror of the Zygons Photograph © BBC Video - Art © Mick Austin

NAME: The Zygons

PLANET OF ORIGIN: Unknown

KNOWN ALLIES: The Skarasen

KNOWN ENEMIES: The Doctor; UNIT

BASE OF OPERATIONS: Their crippled space ship hidden under Loch Ness, Scotland

FIRST APPEARANCE: *Terror of the Zygons*

The Zygons are an amphibious space-travelling race, now scattered across the galaxy in a collection of spaceships. They fled their planet when it became uninhabitable after a natural disaster, seeking new worlds to colonise and eventually reshape into images of their original home.

One of their spaceships crash landed on Earth and for many years the Zygons hid, planning their eventual take over of the planet. They studied humanity carefully and realised that with their chameleon-like metamorphic powers they could infiltrate governments and dominate Earth through political power.

The Doctor discovered them because their cyborg Skarasen, on whom the Zygons relied for nutrients, began destroying oil rigs in and around the North Sea, which was a prelude to their attempt to take control of the planet. Although these Zygons were destroyed, the threat of further invasions cannot be ignored...

Monster File
The AXONS

The Claws of Axos Photograph © BBC Video - The Master Art © Brian Williamson

NAME: The Axons

PLANET OF ORIGIN: Axos

KNOWN ALLIES: The Master

KNOWN ENEMIES: The Doctor; UNIT

BASE OF OPERATIONS: Mobile

FIRST APPEARANCE: *The Claws of Axos*

These shape-changing aliens arrived on Earth resembling golden skinned-aryans. They offered Axonite, a substance that increased an objects mass ten-fold and which could solve Earth's food problems. In return, they requested time and energy to help repair their crippled space ship.

In reality, the Axons were tentacled parasitic monsters, with lethal stings who wanted to suck Earth dry of all its energy before moving on to their next conquest.

They were brought to Earth by the renegade Time Lord the Master, who wanted to destroy the planet in revenge for his previous humiliations. The Doctor tricked the Axons into transporting their ship away from Earth and into space, where he caught them in a time loop, apparently trapping them forever. Whether the Axons ever broke free remains to be seen...

Monster File
The SONTARANS

The Two Doctors Photograph © BBC - Art © David Lloyd

NAME: The Sontarans

PLANET OF ORIGIN: Sontara

KNOWN ALLIES: Vardans; Androgums

KNOWN ENEMIES: The Doctor; Rutans; The Time Lords of Gallifrey

BASE OF OPERATIONS: Mobile

FIRST APPEARANCE: *The Time Warrior*

The Sontarans are a clone species, dedicated to perpetual warring against their equally obsessive enemies, the Rutans.

The war has stretched over many millennia and although casualties have been incalcuable, the Sontaran fleets simply clone and recreate new soldiers as tactics demand.

The Doctor first encountered the Sontarans when one crashed on Earth during the Middle Ages, but by far the most audacious plan they concocted was the attempt to master time by invading Gallifrey, home of the legendary Time Lords. Although they were defeated, the Sontarans have not given up their attempt to destroy the Rutans through time manipulation. Their most recent recorded attempt to gain access to time travel involved them stealing the experimental time capsule from the science Space Station Camera. This plan was initially successful but the Sontarans involved were destroyed without taking the secrets back to their superiors.

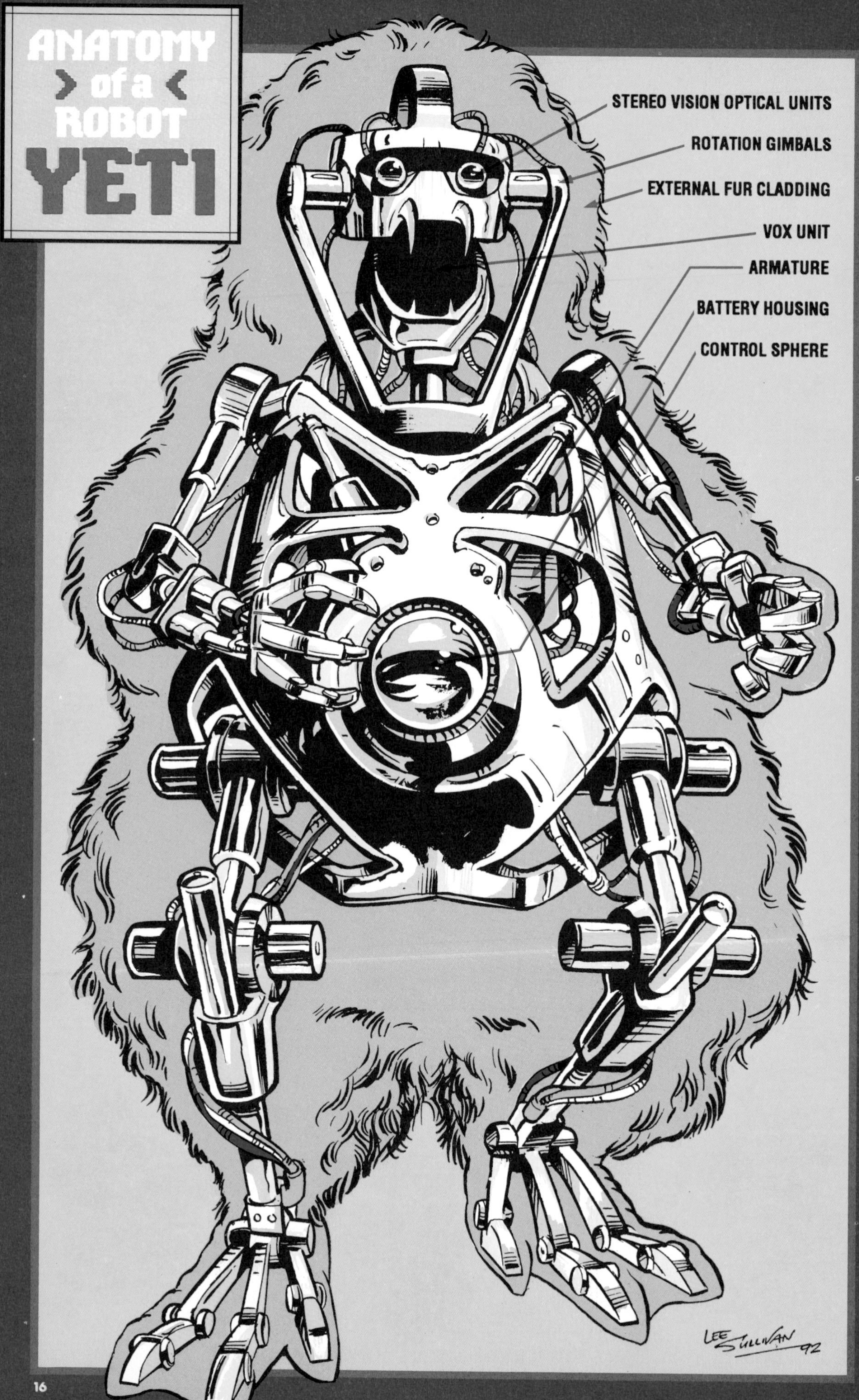

STEREO VISION OPTICAL UNITS

ROTATION GIMBALS

EXTERNAL FUR CLADDING

VOX UNIT

ARMATURE

BATTERY HOUSING

CONTROL SPHERE

LEE SULLIVAN 92

DEEP SPACE. THE FUTURE.

METAMORPHOSIS

PAUL CORNELL (Story) LEE SULLIVAN (Art)
LOUISE CASSELL (Colour) ANNIE H. (Letters)
AND JOHN FREEMAN (Editor) PRESENT—

CAPTAIN, THIS IS *LIDDELL*, CHECKING CARGO BAY TWELVE.

COPY THAT, LIDDELL. KEEP CONTACT, 'KAY?

'KAY.

OH, NO...

CAPTAIN, WE'VE LOST ANOTHER ONE.

POWER LOSS?

NO. I THINK THERE'S—

YEEARRGGHH!

LIDDELL? LIDDELL?

VWORP!
VWORP!

LIDDELL?

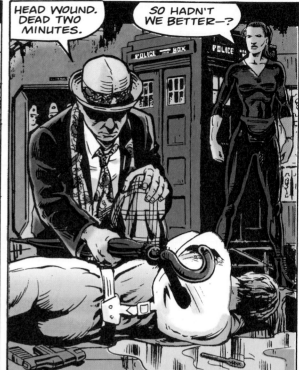

HEAD WOUND. DEAD TWO MINUTES.

SO HADN'T WE BETTER—?

YES. WE'RE UNDER ARREST. WE DIDN'T KILL HIM. TAKE US TO THE BRIDGE.

HEY, D'YOU KNOW WHAT'S GOING ON HERE, DOCTOR?

NOT THIS TIME, ACE...

BUT I SMELL SOMETHING... SOMETHING EVIL.

THAT'S *FIVE* EMBRYOS MISSING AND THREE DEAD CREW...

REALLY?

WHAT'S THE *NAME* OF THIS SHIP?

WHERE'S IT *HEADING?*

THE BIO-FREIGHTER *MITRE*, ON THE WAY TO EARTH. WHO THE HELL ARE *YOU?!*

THESE ARE THE *SUSPECTS*, MA'AM.

OBVIOUSLY. BUT I SEE YOU'VE ALREADY PUT ONE PERSON IN THE BRIG. WHY DO YOU THINK HE WAS STEALING HUMAN EMBRYOS?

DOCTOR HARDING'S IN THE BRIG, BUT HE JUST STRUCK LUCKY. HE'S GOT COMPANY COMING. *GUARDS!*

I'LL BE DOWN TO QUESTION THEM LATER.

BEFORE YOU DO— EXAMINE THE GLASS ON THE BROKEN TANKS!

SO WHY ARE THEY CARRYING A SKIPFUL OF EMBRYOS?

EARTH NEEDS THEM. AFTER THE *DRACONIAN WARS*, THEIR GENETIC POOL'S BECOME A MUDDY PUDDLE.

THESE ARE GROWN ON A BIO-COLONY, GENETICALLY BLANK. IT'S BIG BUSINESS IN THIS TIME PERIOD.

BLANK?

YES. THEY'LL BE IMPRINTED WITH THE GENES OF THEIR *FOSTER PARENTS*. VALUABLE LITTLE CREATURES. THE CAPTAIN OBVIOUSLY THOUGHT HARDING WANTED TO *SELL* THEM ON THE BLACK MARKET.

PROFESSOR...

SHH. WE'RE HERE.

GRRRR...

OH, GREAT.

HE'S SUFFERED A VAST TRAUMA. TOTALLY WITHDRAWN.

THAT SMELL... IS IT?

IT'S ME. *NUMISMATON GAS.* MY TISSUES ARE *MUTATING.*

BUT WHY?

I DUNNO ABOUT YOUR PERSONAL HYGIENE, PROFESSOR, BUT I THINK THIS GUY'S TRYING TO TELL YOU SOMETHING...

EGGS... STIR...

MAYBE HE CAN SMELL YOU TOO, EH?

DOCTOR...

I HAD THE SHARDS EXAMINED—THE FLASK WAS BROKEN FROM THE *INSIDE.* I DON'T KNOW WHO YOU ARE BUT YOU SEEM LIKE MY BEST SHOT AT SOLVING THIS— WHAT DO YOU WANT FROM *ME?*

I NEED ACCESS TO YOUR *MEDICAL LAB.* OH, AND I HAVE A JOB FOR *ACE* AS WELL...

LATER—

FIVE? IS THAT ALL?

THERE ISN'T A BIG CREW ON THESE SHIPS— IT'S MAINLY AUTOMATED.

OH WELL, AT LEAST WE'VE GOT A GUIDE...

EGGS!

IN THE MEDICAL LAB—

WELL, DOCTOR, WHAT'S HAPPENING TO MY CARGO?

I'M MORE WORRIED ABOUT WHAT'S HAPPENING TO ME...

TIME LORD BODIES ARE VERY MALLEABLE UNDER THE RIGHT CONDITIONS. THEY CAN BE AFFECTED BY CERTAIN THINGS AS EASILY AS AN... EMBRYO. ON A CELLULAR LEVEL, I'M CHANGING. IT'S AS IF I CAN HEAR A... SIGNAL...

ACTIVATE THE DISTRESS BEACON! ALL FREQUENCIES!

DONE!

EMERGENCY

BEAC

EEEEEEE!

NOW WOULD YOU MIND TELLING ME WHY, DOCTOR...

ELSEWHERE—

WHAT'S IN THERE?

AIRLOCK.

LET'S HAVE A LOOK.

BE CAREFUL... WE COULD BE IN FOR—

TROUBLE!

SKREEE!

WH-- GLEARRCHKK!

FALL BACK! FALL BACK!

SCH-TOOM!

IN THE LAB—

EGGS... STIR...

WARNING AIRLOCK DOOR OPEN

KTHUNK!

EGGS! STIR!

23

CONTINUED ON PAGE 47!

BRIEF ENCOUNTER

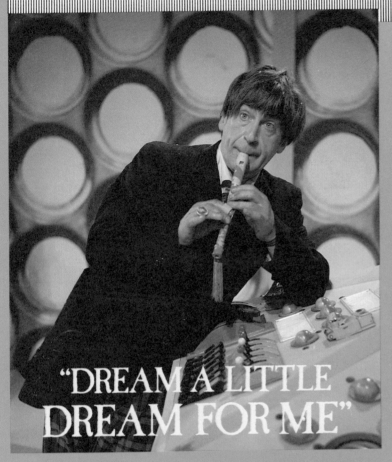

"DREAM A LITTLE DREAM FOR ME"

The tea's getting cold. C'mon Zoe, we've got work to do!"
The words filtered into Zoe Herriot's mind, like a fond memory from long ago. The familiar voice was one that she'd never thought she'd hear again.

Slowly, she opened her eyes. Sure enough, looking over her was that same old face, jade-green eyes sparkling. The little man grinned from ear to ear like a Cheshire cat, and he clasped his hands in delight.

"There! I knew you'd wake up eventually!"

Zoe sat up and raised a hand to her forehead; she had a terrible headache. "Doctor? Where are we? What am I doing here?"

"Well, to answer your questions in order: yes; in a space station; and you've been very ill."

"Ill? What do you mean, ill?"

The little man's face fell. "Well, I suppose it was really my fault..." he said sheepishly.

"Was it... Was it the Time Lords?"

The little man frowned. "Time Lords? What are you talking about?"

"The Time Lords," Zoe repeated. "They sent me back to my own time. Don't you remember?"

The little man shook his head.

"Time Lords? Never heard of 'em!"

"But they're your own... Oh, never mind," she said. If the Doctor was going to be enigmatic that was his own problem.

"What happened?"

"You had a little accident, I'm afraid. I should have known better than to link you into the TARDIS' telepathic circuits when your mind was untrained. You couldn't handle the shock. Your mind switched itself off..."

"You mean I've been in some sort of coma?"

The little man nodded guiltily,

"How long?"

"Twenty-three years!"

The little man produced a small mirror from his coat pocket, and Zoe looked at her face. Yes, she *had* aged. There were lines about her eyes and a few streaks of grey in her hair.

"But this is impossible," she said. "You showed me the Daleks, and then we landed on – on Dulkis! Yes, that was it! You *do* remember Dulkis, don't you?"

"Of course," said the little man. "Charming, peaceful place – I visited it with Polly and Ben."

"Well, then we met Brigadier Lethbridge-Stewart..."

"*Colonel* Lethbridge-Stewart," he corrected her.

Zoe ignored him. "Don't you remember the Krotons? Tobias Vaughn? Oh, for heaven's sake, you must remember the War Lord!?"

"Zoe, I don't know what you're talking about. Perhaps you dreamt it all?"

"Of course I haven't!" she retorted, clearly angry at his little game. "Look, where's Jamie? He'll tell you!"

"Jamie left shortly after you fell into a coma," the little man said. "He's raising sheep in Yorkshire now."

"He always was the freewheeling type," Zoe agreed. "But tell me exactly what happened."

"Well, after that nasty business with the Cybermen on the Wheel, I linked you up to the TARDIS telepathic circuits to give you a foretaste of what might happen if you were to travel with me and Jamie," said the Doctor. "You *do* remember that, don't you?"

"Of course."

"Well, it seems that your mind and the TARDIS' were... incompatible."

"That's hardly surprising," said Zoe. "It's not the most logical of creations. Like K9 said, it's a very stupid machine..." Her voice trailed off, and she frowned. Something was wrong here. How could she know about K9?

"So you blanked out," continued the Doctor, ignoring the slight to his time machine. "I've been here on and off for the past twenty-three years waiting for you to wake up. My friend Dastari and his assistants have been looking after you."

"But that's silly!" insisted Zoe. "Dastari's dead – the Sontarans killed him!"

"Sontarans? How do you know about Sontarans?"

"I... I don't know," she flustered, "I suppose Jamie told me before the Time Lords erased my memory of you –"

"But Zoe," the Doctor reproached, "if these Time Lords – whoever *they* are – wiped your memory, how do you remember me, and all these adventures we're supposed to have had?"

Zoe shook her head, sadly. "You're right, I can't have remembered that," she said. "I suppose you're right after all... the Krotons, the Space Pirates, the Quarks, I must have made them all up..."

The Doctor patted her head sympathetically. "Perhaps the TARDIS opened up the creative, emotional side of your mind much more than you realised," he suggested. "Still, it's

25

odd that you should know Dastari's dead."

"Why's that?"

"I had a similar dream a few nights ago," he revealed. "In fact, I've been having the oddest dreams lately. Keep on bumping into the strangest collection of misfits, all of whom are pretending to be me. That one with the white hair and frilly shirt is particularly annoying, quite disconcerting really... got stranded on a place called Gallifrey. Ever heard of it?"

Zoe looked strangely at the Doctor. "Probably some place in Ireland," she lied, and remembered a toothy, curly-haired man in a long scarf from her dreams who said exactly the same thing. "So what do I do now!?"

"As soon as you're better, I'll take the TARDIS out of storage and we'll be off on our travels again. There's a wonderful universe out there, Zoe, full of the most incredible sights, where the seas are asleep, the sands are singing and people are made of smoke..."

"Someone else said something very similar a long time ago..."

"A very poetic chap, whoever he was," said the Doctor as he turned to leave. "I must go and get the TARDIS now," he continued, and then added:

"Although with the financial mess this space station is in, I wouldn't be surprised if they haven't auctioned it off by now! If you want anything, Nurse Zodin is just outside."

When he had left, Zoe settled back down onto her pillow. Suddenly she sat upright as she noticed for the first time another person in the room. She was *sure* he hadn't been there before.

"'Which dreamed it?'" quoted the stranger, and closed his first-edition copy of *Through the Looking Glass and What Alice Found There.*

"Who are you?" asked Zoe.

"Oh, I'm a doctor," he said, and Zoe could detect a faint Scottish burr in his voice. "Has that other Doctor been bothering you?"

"No," she replied. "Excuse me, haven't we met somewhere before?"

"Not yet..." he said, mysteriously. "He gets a little confused sometimes, poor chap. All that messing around with the time lines, I suppose... But how are *you* feeling?"

"Confused," she admitted. "All these things I dreamt – well, at least I *suppose* I dreamt. My head feels like it wants to burst!"

"You just need a little therapy, that's all," said the stranger. "Why not try writing down everything you remember?" he pointed at an old fashioned typewriter on a desk in the corner. "It usually helps, you know – at least, that's what Carl Gustav told me."

He stood up and made for the door. "I have to go now. I've a young friend who's just discovered this station's chemistry lab. I must find her before she blows us all up..." There was a sudden look of concern – *or was it desperation?* – on his face. "Now you *will* write down all you remember – *all* your dreams – won't you? There's a lot of us depending on you, you know..."

"I promise," Zoe said.

When the little man had left, she got out of bed and went over to the desk where she slipped a piece of paper into the antiquated typewriter.

She already had a story, scores of stories in fact; all she needed now was a title for the first one.

Smiling, she tapped out on the keys:

THE DOMINATORS
Episode 1

Nigel Robinson

COLLECTORS' CORNER

The Silly Season

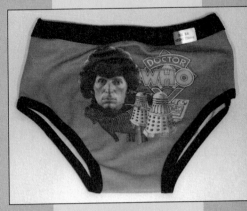

The Dalek Pocketbook and Space-Travellers Guide
Publisher: Souvenir Press/ Panther Books
Year: 1965
Price: 2/6d

Why are Daleks so stupid? I wondered long and hard as to the answer to that question. Their foolishness is matched only by their incompetence when it came to war. Why, you would almost think they had been invented by a half-mad, half-blind wizened old loony with only one arm who spent his life in a wheelchair! To top it all, one of the facts presented in this book is that Daleks cannot see the colour red. This means that in an invasion they would be bumping in to post boxes, old phone boxes and mail delivery vans, as well as not being able to see their commanders, who were red in colour (one of which is even shown on the cover).

Doctor Who Underpants
Manufacturer: British Home Stores
Year: 1981
Price: 85p

One thing that I have never been able to work out is why Doctor Who Underpants form the epitome of all that is silly about the merchandise. Surely there are sillier things . . . the Dalek plastic sheeting, for example, or what about the Dalek Hat, or even the Doctor Who combined nose-hair clipper and sun shade – you hadn't heard of that? Well don't blame me! In fact, the underpants had a very practical and worthwhile use, and only a loony would wear them outside his trousers for all to see.

Junior Doctor Who Books
Publisher: W H Allen
Year: 1980
Price: 75p/85p

Junior Doctor Who went down on one knee in the corridor leading to the gym.
"Hmm," he murmured to himself, inspecting the scuff marks on the polished wooden floor.
His companion, Sarah, a wide eyed girl of about twelve, looked at his puzzled expression. "What is it Doctor?" she asked, the beginnings of a nasal whine creeping through her voice.
"This is just the beginning!" the Doctor muttered, more to himself than to her. "Come on." He bounded to his feet and stalked off down the corridor, pausing at the entrance to the gym. "If we're quick, we may be able to save some." With this he poked his head around the gym door, and raced inside, scarf flying.
What could it be, thought his companion. Alien monsters perhaps, or a race in peril. The Doctor was prone to all manner of fanciful notions.

There was a thump from the room, followed by a muttered cursing and mumbling.
"As I suspected," the Doctor announced loudly.
Sarah poked her head round the door, and saw that the Doctor was standing by the tea trolley, happily munching at a cheese sandwich, while holding a plate of chocolate cake in the other. The tea-lady, Elsie was pinned to the floor by the Doctor's foot, her legs entangled in his long scarf.
"Another case solved, my dear," said the Doctor around a mouthful of bread and cheese. "Help yourself!"

Fifth Doctor Jigsaws
Manufacturer: Waddingtons
Year: 1982
Price: £1.50 each

"What are you doing in my TARDIS?"
"I'm not in your TARDIS, I'm in another photo!"
"Oh."
"By the way, you're not in this photo either!"
"Good grief, so I'm not. And what's more, this isn't even a real TARDIS console, it's a painting!"
"What devilish swine has done this to us?!"
"Tell you what."
"What?"
"There's another three jigsaws just like this!"
"Oh no!!"

David J Howe

27

BRIEF ENCOUNTER

COUNTRY of the BLIND

Watch it!" The Doctor ducked as the new captain shouted, his head narrowly missing the end of a ladder. On the end of the ladder swung a pot of paint. The Doctor stood again, irritated.

"Captain . . . whatever your name is –"

"Yates, Doctor. Michael."

"Could you please decorate the lab at some other time. I'm in the middle of a very important thought experiment." He tapped his skull meaningfully.

"Sorry, Doc. The Brig wants to brighten the place up. Good for morale."

The Doctor made an indignant noise. He'd been considering his new incarnation, his newfound prowess at the martial arts. It was as if his body wasn't gaining new skills but . . . remembering them.

Liz Shaw strode in, her expression a mixture of nervousness and amusement.

"Ah, there you are m'dear. Perhaps you can help me –"

"Doctor, we have to talk . . ."

"Absolutely. Tell me, do you believe in reincarnation?"

The ladder-bearers tottered towards a delicate experiment, and the Doctor and Liz leapt forward to save it.

"No," muttered Liz. "Listen, Doctor . . . I've had an offer from Queen Mary . . ."

"I had one of those once. She wanted me to be her court physician.

Had to turn her down . . ." The Doctor rubbed his nose and grinned.

"This is serious. They want me to work at CERN, the new research facility. It would mean leaving UNIT."

"What? Well, you don't want to do that, do you? Oh, I say, mind those test-tubes!"

Liz looked down at the floor, quietly fuming as the Doctor strode over to the soldiers and made a couple of imperious gestures. If she stayed, it would be because of the knowledge in his head, all that delicious alien data. Not that she'd heard anything concerning alien worlds beyond anecdotes about Perigosto Sticks. The stituation wasn't fair on either of them.

He wandered back over, and put a finger under her chin. "Chin up, eh? There'll be other offers . . ."

"I'm taking this one." She met his gaze steadily, her eyes briefly flashing resentment. "I was considering staying, but you've convinced me. I have a brilliant career in front of me, Doctor. I have to put that first."

"Yes," the Doctor frowned. "Yes, I suppose you must. This must seem like some sort of circus to you . . ."

Liz softened. She'd struck him too hard. But that's what happened to people who used confidence to hide their vulnerability. She should know. "A great circus, Doctor. Full of sound and fury . . ."

"Signifying nothing," his voice was quite empty. "Best thing Will ever wrote . . ."

There was a crash. The Doctor spun around, livid. "That's valuable equipment!" he yelled. "This is really intolerable, let me see . . ."

He looked over his shoulder as he marched forward, intending to ask Liz to at least share a final glass of wine.

But she was gone. The door swung meaninglessly at her passing.

The Doctor rubbed the back of his neck, pondering.

"Well, Doctor, what do you want us to do?" asked the captain who had been watching events with some bemusement.

"Oh . . . whatever you think best, old chap. And please, m'dear fellow, can I call you Mike?"

Mike Yates smiled, and picked up a pot of paint.

When the Brigadier found him, the Doctor was meditating, eyes closed. The Soldier approached the Time Lord warily, aware that in the past, their encounters had been aggressive and pointed. "Doctor, something's come up. Man in Kent says he's got fairies at the bottom of his garden."

The Doctor opened his eyes. He smiled a different smile. "Brigadier, I have better things to . . . No, no I haven't, as a matter of fact. Sit down, old chap, and tell me what the situation is."

The Brigadier sat down, not attempting a lotus.

And after a while, he found himself smiling too.

Paul Cornell

Daggers of the MIND

Doctor Who has not only seen alien invasions of planets: the human mind has also proved a fertile ground for deadly possession – and the attacks on free will by many different beings, including the Doctor's arch enemy, the Master, have equally taken many very different forms.

Photo © BBC

Perhaps the most damaging of invasions, as far as the individual is concerned, is an invasion of the mind. Minds have been invaded almost throughout the history of *Doctor Who*; sometimes the victims have been overwhelmed by the assault, sometimes they have fought back and regained some, or all, of their personality and self-will.

From the Sensorites' inadvertent invasion of the human mind (the

spaceship crew member, John), through to the possession of Ace by the strange planet of the Cheetah People, 'the enemy within' has been a recurring theme in *Doctor Who*. It has often served to show the resilience and persistence of the human mind and the power of self-will.

Possibly the most common form of mind invasion is hypnotism. Renegade Time Lord, and the Doctor's greatest foe, the Master has been responsible

for numerous hypnotisms, right from his first appearance in the 1971 story *Terror of the Autons*. When he appears in his twelfth, and apparently final, regeneration in *The Deadly Assassin* (broadcast in 1976) he again wastes no time in using his power to help him control Time Lord Chancellor Goth and Chancellory Guard Solis. Similarly, when, during his attempt to rejuvenate his dying form in *The Keeper of Traken* (1980), he hypnotises Tremas from inside his Melkur-disguised TARDIS and forces him to kill Proctor Neman. Having taken over the body of Tremas, he uncharacteristically controls Nyssa via a wrist bracelet rather than through pure hypnosis in 1981's *Logopolis*. However, by the 1982 story *Time-Flight* he is back to his old tricks!

The Master's hypnotism, however, is flawed. Some of the stronger willed of his intended victims can resist. The Doctor's companion Jo Grant has taught herself a resistance technique by 1973's *Frontier in Space* and the Master is completely unable to influence, amongst others Miss Hawthorne in *The Dæmons* (1971), CPO Smedley in *The Sea Devils* (1972) or John Farrel in *Terror of the Autons* (1971). According to the Doctor, the minds of those he *does* hypnotise struggle to resist as soon as they have got well away from the Master.

A more complete form of hypnosis than the Master's is the mind control used by Eldrad in another 1976 story, *The Hand of Fear*. Focussed through his ring, the Kastrian criminal uses it initially to enslave Sarah Jane Smith, the Doctor's companion. After her, Dr Carter and a technician called Driscoll fall under his power. Another renegade Time Lord and contemporary of the Doctor, the Rani, seems to have also moved to more physical means of mind control – chemically-impregnated parasites which the victim is forced to swallow, as seen in the 1985 story *The Mark of the Rani*. Time Lord President Borusa, in the 1983 celebratory adventure *The Five Doctors* even takes total control of the Doctor's mind – although this control is augmented by the Coronet of Rassilon. ▶

In *The Five Doctors*, Borusa (Philip Latham) extends his power via the Coronet of Rassilon. Photo © BBC Video

More insidious is a control of the perception, such as the Master's manipulation of the minds of both humans and Draconians in *Frontier in Space*. They see what they most fear – and their fear of each other is what brings them to the brink of war. On a greater scale is the control of the inhabitants of the city of Morphoton in the 1964 serial *The Keys of Marinus*. The people see their city as beautiful, clean and luxurious – in fact it is squalid, decaying and rat-infested.

This is somewhat similar to the control exerted over the colonists by the Macra in the 1967 story *The Macra Terror*, and in *The War Games* (1969), the Alien kidnappers of soldiers from throughout Earth's history control their captives' perception so they believe they are still fighting their own wars.

ALTERED PERCEPTIONS

The crew of the *SS Bernice* in 1973's *Carnival of Monsters* have their perceptions altered by Vorg's miniscope. Not only do they believe that they are still on their ship in the Indian Ocean (despite the fact it is broad daylight even though it should be dark) but they can be *further* manipulated. Vorg heightens their emotions at one point via controls on the miniscope and even the Doctor is affected, facing Lieutenant Andrews in a bare-fisted fight.

This is a form of remote control, similar – if cruder – to the way the Zarbi and their controller, the Animus, manipulate people who are in contact with gold in 1965's *The Web Planet*. The Zarbi are able to entice Barbara, one of the Doctor's companions, from the TARDIS because of the golden bracelet she wears (which she was given by Roman Emperor Nero in an earlier adventure).

The supercomputer WOTAN in the 1966 story *The War Machines* exerts a remote control over its victims – particularly its creator Professor Brett and his secretary Polly. Channing's

Photo © BBC Video

In the 1973/4 adventure *The Time Warrior*, Linx the Sontaran's control of the twentieth century scientists he transports back to medieval England is also breakable, with the Doctor's help. He reverses the optical conditioning with a repeated sequence of flashing light. The giant spiders of Metebelis 3 control their prey more through mental pain than technology. If the treacherous human, Lupton, resists them, in 1974's *Planet of the Spiders*, then they make him feel as if red hot needles are being pushed into his mind – a trick he later discovers he can reverse, and attacks the spiders!

The Shadow's control of the Atrion Marshal in 1979's *The Armageddon Factor* is definitely technologically augmented, by a control box on the Marshal's neck. However, whether the Marshal is a victim or a willing servant –helping the Shadow in order to guarantee victory – is not clear. But the humans, controlled in a similar manner by the Terileptils in 1982's *The Visitation* (the control device this time being on the wrist) are not willing servants.

The master and slave relationship between the Black Guardian and the Doctor's companion Turlough is less clear cut. In the 1983 story *Mawdryn Undead* it seems that Turlough is keen to help the Guardian kill the Doctor – although he struggles to avoid the issue, more through cowardice than morality! Similarly, one senses that an understanding of sorts has also been reached between the performers of the Psychic Circus and their controllers, the Gods of Ragnarok, in 1988's *The Greatest Show in the Galaxy*. Other not-entirely-unwilling slaves are Lady Pritchard and her daughter Gwendoline who, the Doctor comments, enjoy their evil rôles too much in 1989's *Ghostlight*.

Arthur Terrall in *The Evil of the Daleks* (1967) does not enjoy his rôle as a pawn of the Daleks; he is never controlled as absolutely as the Dalek-factored Theodore Maxtible. Terrall does however have to endure the sounds of the Dalek commands within his struggling brain, an inability (and presumably lack of need) to eat, and a body that the Doctor discovers is charged up with static electricity.

The Cybermen, too, take over humans when it suits them. They control the humans on *The Moonbase* (1967) through the use of a headset – not unlike their human servants in 1988's *Silver Nemesis*. In *The Wheel in Space* (1968), an electrical charge to their victim's head suffices. The Cybermen's technique seems to make for total control of the subject – more akin to the way the Daleks control the Robomen of Twenty-Second century

Cybermen, regular users of mind control over their human victims. *Silver Nemesis* Photo © BBC

Lady Pritchard (Sylvia Syms) seemed to enjoy her villainy a little too much! *Ghost Light* Photo © BBC

control over Hibbert in *Spearhead from Space* (1970) may also be of this type. Hibbert, however, is able to break the control and rebel – until Channing has him killed by an Auton.

Earth in *The Dalek Invasion of Earth* (1964), though the Robomen do revert to humanity for one final gesture – their suicide! The bulky headger used to control the Robomen is not needed, however, to control the Headmaster or the schoolgirl from Coal Hill School in 1988's *Remembrance of the Daleks*. Perhaps the Daleks of the future have perfected the technique?

PSYCHIC LINKS

To control Sir George Hutchinson in 1984's *The Awakening*, the Malus seems to use psychic energy rather than machinery. Likewise, the possession of the Chief Caretaker of *Paradise Towers* (1987) by Kroagnon, the Great Architect, and Romana's possession by the instincts and pain of the Marsh Child in 1980's *Full Circle* are both more biological than technological. Possession to the extent that the victim's mind is all but lost is a common theme. The Great Intelligence controls Padmasambhava (*The Abominable Snowmen*, 1967), Sergeant Arnold and, for a while, Professor Travers and Victoria Waterfield (*The Web of Fear*, 1968) in this manner. Similarly, Sutekh is able to control the Doctor completely in 1975's *Pyramids of Mars*, only relaxing control when he thinks the Doctor is dead – ironic since he controls the body of Marcus Scarman *after* he has killed the explorer!

Whether Hieronymous and the Brotherhood of Demnos are 'alive' after they have been totally possessed by the Mandragora Helix is uncertain in 1976's *The Masque of Mandragora*. The process of their possession probably kills them, just as the implantation of Kiv's brain in Peri certainly destroys her (or would have done if it had actually happened in 1986's *The Trial of a Time Lord!*).

A strange form of physical, as well as mental, possession takes over the shape-changing android Kamelion in 1984's *Planet of Fire*. Firstly, he assumes the form of Professor Howard Foster (although he struggles to resist) and later that of his controller – once again, the Master! The strange forces exerted by the planet of the Cheetah people mutate the body as well as the mind into a Cheetah Person in *Survival* (1989) and the mutation of the infected technicians and soldiers at Project Inferno is predominantly physical, although the mind also seems to revert to the primeval in 1970's *Inferno*. In 1975's *Planet of Evil*, Professor Sorenson undergoes a transformation similar to this as he is possessed, firstly for short periods of time, then completely by the antimatter of Zeta Minor.

Reversion to unreasoning animal is also, paradoxically, the effect of being stung by one of the Varga plants of the planet Skaro – transplanted to Kembel by the Daleks. As seen in 1965's *Mission to the Unknown*, the brain is destroyed and the body slowly

Above top: The Chief Caretaker (Richard Briers), under the influence of Kroagnon, the Great Archtiect of *Paradise Towers*. Photo © BBC. Middle: Arnold Keeler becomes a Krynoid in *The Seeds of Doom*. Photo © BBC. Inset: A Yeti robot, slave of The Great Intelligence in *The Abominable Snowmen*. Photo © BBC. Below: Kamelion, disguised as the Master (Anthony Ainley) on Sarn. *Planet of Fire* Photo © BBC

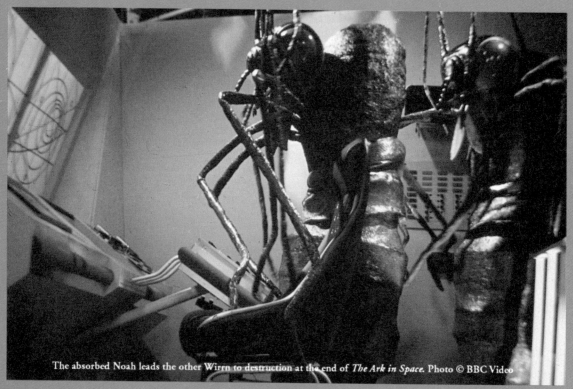

The absorbed Noah leads the other Wirrn to destruction at the end of *The Ark in Space*. Photo © BBC Video

transforms into a Varga itself. A similar process befalls Winlett and Keeler in 1976's *The Seeds of Doom* as they mutate into the Krynoid plant, and their minds are also possessed. Harrison Chase is able to keep his human body – although his mind is invaded and (to his delight) possessed by the Krynoid.

Physical change is often an indication that the mind has been invaded. The human whose body is taken over by *Meglos* (1980) not only changes to resemble the Doctor, thus allowing Meglos to impersonate him, but as the human struggles to resist, Meglos reverts to the human's form – bristling with Meglos' own cactus-like green skin and spines. Possession by the seaweed parasite in 1968's *Fury from the Deep* leads to slight changes in outward appearances for Robson and the others as seaweed grows on their faces, and destroys the self-will of other victims like Oak and Quill.

RESISTANCE IS USEFUL

The most extreme case of a human struggling against mental and physical possession in *Doctor Who* is probably Noah in the 1975 story *The Ark in Space*. Noah's mind is invaded not only by the Wirrn themselves, but by the residual mind of Technician Dune, a previous Wirrn victim. As his body mutates into a Wirrn, and Noah tries to deny the transformation and then fight it, his mind is also invaded and absorbed. The final evidence of a residual spark of humanity is his destruction of the transport ship he has led the Wirrn into.

This resistance of humanity to the

invasion of the mind is a major theme of the series. Just as the Doctor and Bellal resist the Exxilon city's assault on their sanity (*Death to the Daleks*, 1974), so Toberman struggles to resist the mechanical and mental invasion of his body by the Cybermen (*The Tomb of the Cybermen*, 1967). The scientist, Stengos resists Davros' surgery and begs his daughter to kill him before he is completely transformed into a Dalek (*Revelation of the Daleks*, 1985) and the Doctor – that arch exponent of the humanity he lacks – struggles to resist and reduce the probing telepathic intrusion of his mind by the Vardans (*The Invasion of Time*, 1978). Like so many of these possessions of the mind, this is not an actual invasion. The actual, apparently physical, assault within the mind, like that by

The Mara returned to haunt Tegan Jovanka in *Snakedance*. Photo © BBC

the Mara on Tegan in *Kinda* (1982) and against Lon and Tegan in *Snakedance* (1983) is rare in *Doctor Who*.

This concept has been explored in those two Mara stories and in the 1977 story *The Invisible Enemy* (originally entitled *The Enemy Within*). In each case, beings appear to the victim (and the audience) as a physical entity within the mindscape. Dukkha, Anatta and Anicca appear to Tegan in her sleep in *Kinda*, and she confronts the skull of the snake when she looks into a distorting mirror or a crystal ball in *Snakedance*. When the miniaturized clone of the Doctor is injected into his brain in *The Invisible Enemy*, it discovers the black mass of the nucleus of the Virus writhing

The Doctor and Leela search the Doctor's brain for the Nucleus of the Swarm in *The Invisible Enemy*. Photo © BBC

around inside his brain, waving a claw and debating the ethics of the invasion!

There have been many other instances of mind-manipulation, although whether the control of the Master of Fiction in *The Mind Robber* (1968) is an invasion could be debated either way. Similarly, 1971's *The Mind of Evil* takes the image of the victim's worst fear and uses it to kill him or her (more than just the image in fact –

supercomputer BOSS in *The Green Death* (1973) could be explored in depth, and it can be debated which of them ultimately controls the other. BOSS seems to be in charge of Stevens, until the human destroys the computer – a single tear rolling down his cheek as he sits in the control complex waiting for the building to explode around him.

Another interesting twist of the

Eden, 1979) or even stolen (*Shada*, 1979), but for every takeover, for every will subjected to evil control, *Doctor Who* has always seen humans and other races struggle to shake off such influences. Perhaps the final comment on the resilience and independence of the mind is the 1982 story *Castrovalva*. There, the Master has created an entire world and populated it with people whose only purpose for existing is to trap the Doctor and serve the Master. Yet, they rebel; and eventually they turn on and seem to destroy their creator. Their Librarian, Shardovan learns the truth and finally understands the concept of free will when he says: "You made us, man of evil, but we are free" as he heroically destroys both himself and the Master's hold over the Doctor. Just as control and power over the mind is one theme in *Doctor Who*, so is the capacity to resist that terrible threat . . .

Justin Richards

Barnum (Neil McCarthy) becomes the first victim of *The Mind of Evil*. Photo © BBC

Professor Kettering's lungs are full of *water* after he has apparently drowned in the *dry* Process Room in Stangmoor Prison). Do the duplicates created by the Daleks in *Resurrection of the Daleks* (1984) have minds to be invaded and controlled? Perhaps they do, after all Stien seems to revert to his former personna after breaking the Daleks' conditioning.

The symbiotic mental relationship between Stevens and the

invasion of the mind is the 1966 story *The Savages*, where the Elders of the planet drain the minds of the Savages and use the mental energy to augment themselves. A sort of inverse invasion; certainly Jano, leader of the Elders, repents when he steals some of the Doctor's mental energy, and his mind is 'invaded' by the Doctor's morality.

In other stories, minds are destroyed by drugs (*Nightmare of*

Had the Doctor and Peri (Nicola Bryant) really suffered on Thoros Beta as the Matrix suggested in *The Trial of a Time Lord*, the Doctor's companion would have been unlikely to survive the mind transference with the Mentor, Kiv. Photo © BBC

The Daleks, past masters in the art of total mind control, especially in *The Evil of The Daleks*. Photo © BBC

Farewells

I t happened, of all times, on the day they buried the cat. Sarah and K9 stood silent by the little grave at the end of the cottage garden.

Sarah sniffed. Behind her a voice said, "Tears, Sarah Jane?"

She whirled round. "It's you! The you you!"

The Doctor grinned, and pushed his broad-brimmed soft hat to the back of his head. "That's right. All teeth and curls as usual."

Sarah blushed. "I never... oh, yes I did. Who told you?"

"I did!"

"What are you doing here?"

He shrugged. "Oh, just time out." He bent down and patted the robot dog at Sarah's side. "And how are you, K9?"

K9 was silent for a moment – except, that is, for a series of whirrs and clicks. Then he said, "Video circuits, fully functional, Master!

Minor functional deficiency in left audio installation. Mobility running at seventeen per cent below full capability..."

"No need for a full operation check," said the Doctor hurriedly. "I meant, just generally speaking..."

"In general terms – as well as can be expected, Master!"

"Splendid! And you, Sarah Jane?"

"I suppose I could say the same. Why have you come back?"

"To say goodbye. I felt I made rather a botch of it, the first time."

Sarah looked up at him. "Yes," she said fiercely, "you certainly did."

The Doctor nodded towards the little patch of freshly-turned earth. "I seem to have come at rather a bad time."

Sarah blinked away a tear. "Poor old mog handing in his supper dish? He was very old you know. I inherited him from my aunt when she died –

and he was old then."

"But you're still upset?"

"Well, I knew him from a kitten. I remember Aunt Emily getting him when I was a kid. Little scrap of a thing, all ears and feet, bouncing round everywhere." Sarah sighed. "Not now, though. He just lay on the sofa like a great furry cushion. He only got up for his meals – and this morning he didn't get up at all..."

"Brothers and Sisters, I bid you beware Of giving your heart to a dog to tear..." said the Doctor.

"What?"

"Rudyard Kipling – poem about losing a dog. Same thing, really. You have to be careful who you love. Nice chap, old Rudders, though he could be a bit tetchy. I remember once I said to him, 'Rudders', I said, 'you're just too excitable. Now, if you can keep your head when all about you are losing theirs and blaming it on you...' 'Hang on,' he said, 'I'll just jot that down–'"

Sarah interrupted him. "Why did you? Make such a botch of saying goodbye, I mean? You bustled me out of the TARDIS as if it was a Number Nine Bus at the end of the line." She snorted. "No aliens on Gallifrey! Strict anti-immigration rules in those days, were there?"

"Perhaps it was..."

"Was *what?!*"

"The end of the line."

"You could have taken me with you, if you'd wanted to."

"No, Sarah Jane. I couldn't take you with me *because* I wanted to."

"But we could have gone on –"

"Not forever," said the Doctor.

Sarah looked at him. She looked at the flower bed that held the mortal remains of Mog. "Ah," she said.

The Doctor took her hand, held it for a moment, kissed it and let it go. "Goodbye, Sarah Jane. I'm sorry..."

"Nothing to be sorry about, Doctor. We had some times, didn't we?"

"Time and time again," said the Doctor. "It never ends, you know, not really. Goodbye, K9."

"Goodbye, Master."

The Doctor turned, strode to the end of the garden, vaulted lightly over the fence and disappeared into the trees. Sarah caught a flash of police box blue and heard a wheezing, groaning sound...

"Come along K9," said Sarah quietly.

"Mistress?"

Sarah realised she was addressing his deaf ear and moved to the other side. "I said come on! We can't stand here mooning over an ex-moggie. I've got things to do! I'm not getting any younger you know!"

"Mistress?"

Sarah strode briskly up the path. A little slowly, a little creakily, K9 followed.

Terrance Dicks

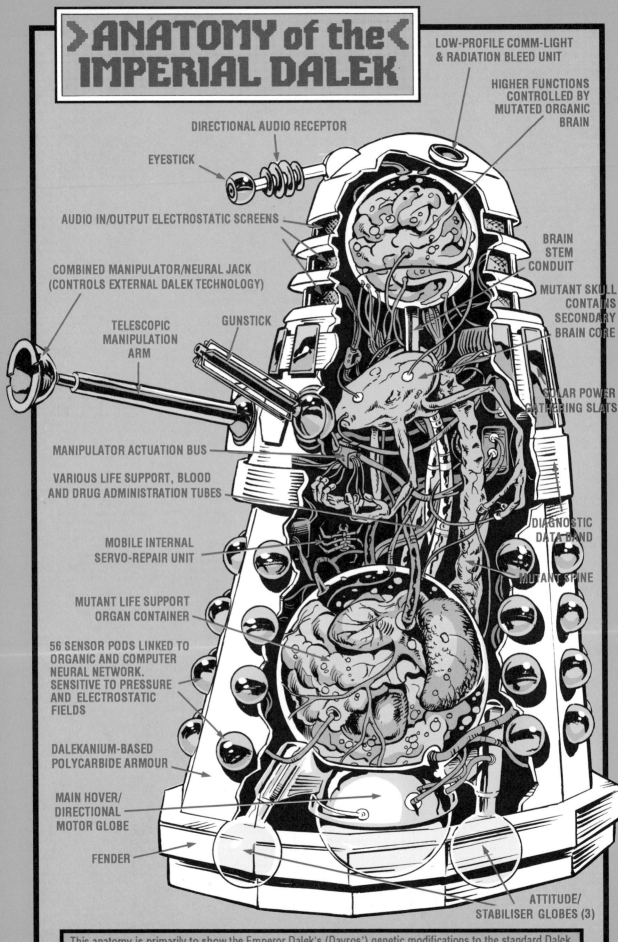

>ANATOMY of the< IMPERIAL DALEK

LOW-PROFILE COMM-LIGHT & RADIATION BLEED UNIT

HIGHER FUNCTIONS CONTROLLED BY MUTATED ORGANIC BRAIN

DIRECTIONAL AUDIO RECEPTOR

EYESTICK

AUDIO IN/OUTPUT ELECTROSTATIC SCREENS

BRAIN STEM CONDUIT

MUTANT SKULL CONTAINS SECONDARY BRAIN CORE

COMBINED MANIPULATOR/NEURAL JACK (CONTROLS EXTERNAL DALEK TECHNOLOGY)

GUNSTICK

TELESCOPIC MANIPULATION ARM

SOLAR POWER GATHERING SLATS

MANIPULATOR ACTUATION BUS

VARIOUS LIFE SUPPORT, BLOOD AND DRUG ADMINISTRATION TUBES

DIAGNOSTIC DATA BAND

MOBILE INTERNAL SERVO-REPAIR UNIT

MUTANT SPINE

MUTANT LIFE SUPPORT ORGAN CONTAINER

56 SENSOR PODS LINKED TO ORGANIC AND COMPUTER NEURAL NETWORK. SENSITIVE TO PRESSURE AND ELECTROSTATIC FIELDS

DALEKANIUM-BASED POLYCARBIDE ARMOUR

MAIN HOVER/ DIRECTIONAL MOTOR GLOBE

FENDER

ATTITUDE/ STABILISER GLOBES (3)

36

This anatomy is primarily to show the Emperor Dalek's (Davros') genetic modifications to the standard Dalek. These modifications were introduced to help quash the renegade Dalek forces in the 'Omega Device' gambit. Circuitry and computer systems have yet to be analysed and therefore are not shown here.

>FUTURE DALEK DESIGN?<

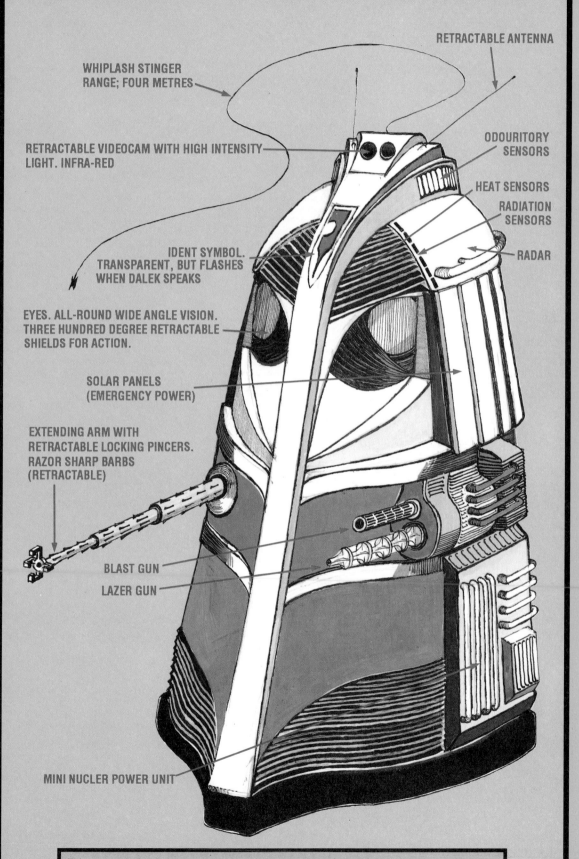

RETRACTABLE ANTENNA

WHIPLASH STINGER
RANGE; FOUR METRES

RETRACTABLE VIDEOCAM WITH HIGH INTENSITY
LIGHT. INFRA-RED

ODOURITORY
SENSORS

HEAT SENSORS

RADIATION
SENSORS

RADAR

IDENT SYMBOL.
TRANSPARENT, BUT FLASHES
WHEN DALEK SPEAKS

EYES. ALL-ROUND WIDE ANGLE VISION.
THREE HUNDRED DEGREE RETRACTABLE
SHIELDS FOR ACTION.

SOLAR PANELS
(EMERGENCY POWER)

EXTENDING ARM WITH
RETRACTABLE LOCKING PINCERS.
RAZOR SHARP BARBS
(RETRACTABLE)

BLAST GUN

LAZER GUN

MINI NUCLER POWER UNIT

This new style Dalek was designed in 1980 by Raymond P Cusick, who designed the original
Daleks for the BBC in 1963. He intends it to look as if it has been constructed from an as-yet
undiscovered metallic substance. The new Dalek stands at approximately 1400 mm high.

MAKING (new) MYTHS

John Nathan-Turner was the producer of *Doctor Who* throughout the Eighties. Recently, he has returned to the worlds of the programme with his productions for BBC Home Video, exploring the past of the show via various 'special' *Doctor Who* releases. Here, John explains just how these 'specials' were created . . .

Photo © John Freeman

When Penny Mills, Head of BBC Home Video Production approached me with regard to extending the Twenty-Sixth season story *The Curse of Fenric*, I had no idea that our association was to be on-going.

Nicholas Mallett (the director of *Fenric*) and I rewatched the original material and the 'first cut' of the individual episodes, to examine the quality of the 'missing' scenes, which had been cut chiefly for reasons of time. It was a slow but rewarding process and as you may know, we were able to reinstate a fair amount of previously un-transmitted material, especially in Part Four.

Incidentally, there never was enough material to make up a fifth episode – the timings did indicate so, but on examining the various takes, it was clear that the programmes were over-length but not quite as dramatically as had been envisaged.

Due to commitments to another project, Nick was unable to attend the final dub of the new extended *Fenric*, so I stood in. Not to do so would have resulted in an expensive remount. As they were delighted with the end results, Ms Mills and her assistant David Jackson took me out to lunch. It was they who approached me with regard to other *Doctor Who* projects, contrary to reports elsewhere. At this lunch, I suggested *The Years Tapes* and *Shada*, but stressed that there was still plenty of material from both complete and incomplete stories still available for release – much of it not seen since its original transmission.

NEW BEGINNINGS

Both projects were preliminarily accepted and it was agreed to start *The Years* series with, appropriately enough, *The Hartnell Years* and *The Troughton Years*. As I started planning, it became obvious I could encompass *The Pertwee Years* in the shoot as well, and therefore save money. However, it was decided to hold back the end results of that recording until March 1992.

In many ways, when deciding which clips and episodes to use, it's more a case of what do you leave out rather than include. Staff at the BBC's Windmill Road Archives, colleagues at BBC Enterprises in general and Home Video in particular have been invaluable with regard to their ideas. Of course, the mail I receive, whenever we announce a 'special' title, many of them using single episodes of incomplete stories from the archives, reflects diverse opinions. Although the decision is ultimately mine, all opinions are taken on board with some included in the end product.

I read a review of these 'special' projects recently which stated that the reviewer didn't know at which market the tapes were aimed. Perhaps I can explain. The projects are aimed at a general market rather than a specific one. We acknowledge that afficionados will probably purchase the tapes in order to get as good a copy (as is available through BBC TV) of the whole episodes contained therein. I am only too aware that any information on the tapes is bound to be already known to every reader of **Doctor Who Magazine** and every member of the *Doctor Who* fan clubs but my brief is clear: "Don't get too bogged down with minutiae and remember clearly the casual purchaser and the nostalgia buyers".

We do attempt, even if we're giving an overview, not to split up whole episodes of complete stories (unlike my infinitives!). In other words, if two episodes of a four part story exist, we will include either a clip or the two *whole* episodes. We wouldn't dream of ▶

The extended version of *The Curse of Fenric* was a successful experiment from BBC Home Video. Photo © BBC Video

Dodo (Jackie Lane) and Steven Taylor (Peter Purves) find themselves up again the Toymaker's minions in *The Celestial Toymaker*. The only surviving episode of this four part story is featured on *The Hartnell Years*. Photo © BBC

Tom Baker reads his script during the recording of the links for *Shada*.
Photo © ARAB

story would be chosen and shown to Tom – as live! We would record his comments with no retakes – if he didn't remember a story, an actor or director, a season even, then so be it! I hope you enjoy the two tapes of *The Tom Baker Years*. Personally, I think that Tom's comments are fascinating and mesmerising.

The Invasion video is much less ambitious but nonetheless effective in its simplicity of presentation.

While Tom was recording his links for *The Tom Baker Years* in the unusual mosaic palace-like surroundings of Leighton House Museum in Holland Park, London, I decided to attempt to shoot an opening link to replace the missing Episode One of *The Invasion* and a further link to cover Episode Four, which also no longer exists.

I had originally hoped to use a totally different room with a super mirror for the links, but time started to evaporate as usual!

I asked Nicholas Courtney to present the package, as his character made its first appearance as 'The Brigadier' as opposed to 'The Colonel' in this yarn. This he did superbly.

It is due for release sometime during 1993.

THE FUTURE

I don't know where the idea of a Daleks and Cybermen video came from: perhaps the Head of Home Videos herself, but I enjoyed writing and producing these projects enormously. The Daleks and Cybermen area of the M and J Media *Behind the Sofa* Exhibition at the Museum of the Moving Image in London (which has

including just a single episode of a partly existing story.

TOM'S PROJECTS

When I approached Tom Baker to complete *Shada*, he was enthusiastic but not so interested in *The Tom Baker Years* project. However, he asked me to think of a "dangerous" way of doing these tapes (with Tom's massive seven year stint to cover, *The Tom Baker Years* was a daunting task anyway!). The idea I came up with appealed to Tom enormously – a clip from each

John Nathan-Turner directs the recording of the *Shada* links at the Museum of the Moving Image on London's South Bank. Photo © ARAB

40

Only one episode of *The Crusade*, starring Julian Glover as Richard the Lionheart, exists. This also features on *The Hartnell Years*. Photo © BBC

now begun a tour around different parts of the British Isles) provided an ideal backdrop for the recording of the links for the tapes, and the enthusiasm of presenters Peter Davison and Colin Baker for the projects at hand is self-evident. It was decided to concentrate on *The Early Years* of these famous creations in order to include as many whole episodes of incomplete Dalek and Cyber stories as possible.

1993 is of course the Thirtieth anniversary of *Doctor Who*. A multitude of ideas is being considered by BBC Home Video Executives to celebrate this milestone in TV history, even if new *Doctor Who* material is not being produced at present. I'm delighted to have been asked to produce the projects.

If I'm free, there's nothing I'd like more! ◆

Nicholas Courtney aka Brigadier Lethbridge-Stewart links *The Invasion*, where two of its eight episodes are still missing. Photo © ARAB

Photo © John Freeman

> The SONIC < SCREWDRIVER

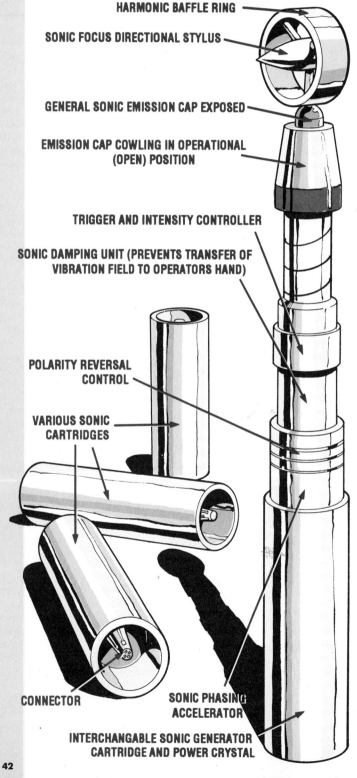

HARMONIC BAFFLE RING

SONIC FOCUS DIRECTIONAL STYLUS

GENERAL SONIC EMISSION CAP EXPOSED

EMISSION CAP COWLING IN OPERATIONAL (OPEN) POSITION

TRIGGER AND INTENSITY CONTROLLER

SONIC DAMPING UNIT (PREVENTS TRANSFER OF VIBRATION FIELD TO OPERATORS HAND)

POLARITY REVERSAL CONTROL

VARIOUS SONIC CARTRIDGES

CONNECTOR

SONIC PHASING ACCELERATOR

INTERCHANGABLE SONIC GENERATOR CARTRIDGE AND POWER CRYSTAL

LEE SULLIVAN '92

"I created the sonic screwdriver," declared former *Doctor Who* script editor Victor Pemberton during an interview in 1989, talking about the Doctor's futuristic device which enabled him to escape (and discover!) many threats to his life. In another interview, regular Seventies director Michael Briant claimed that the famed tool was an inspiration of his during the rehearsals for the first story in which it was used, *Fury from the Deep* in 1968, on which he worked as a production assistant. "It's a sonic screwdriver – never fails!" explained the Doctor to his companions Victoria and Jamie. Standing over a gas pipeline junction box on the cold English coastline in Episode 1, the Doctor made the device emit a high pitched whine. As the tip glowed, a screw in the metal plating was seen to emerge from the casing, all by itself. "There we are. Neat isn't it, hmmm? All done by soundwaves," commented its inventor, smugly.

The original prop, seen in the Patrick Troughton serials, appears to be a simple pen-torch. The first uses – usually shot on film – involved such things as the extraction of screws apparently by their own accord but actually rotated from beneath a hollow prop, out of camera shot or, as in the case of *The Dominators*, it functioned as a metal-cutting flame.

During the Pertwee years the sonic screwdriver gained a new lease of life in the hands of the gadget-crazy Doctor. The shape changed gradually until the familiar silver-barrelled device became the norm, first seen in *The Three Doctors*. Still like the original, but considerably larger, it was now activated by rotating the outer shell. A variety of head pieces appeared to be added on, notably a bulbous red hemisphere in some stories.

The version seen during Tom Baker's tenure underwent many modifications, although it began as the same basic silver prop with the red top used by the previous Doctor. In some stories, such as 1978's *The Pirate Planet*, it was silver and had a black crosswire swivel head activated by an outer sliding sheath. For *The Horns of Nimon* in 1979, the prop bore a silver nozzle head instead and had a rotating barrel action to activate it. It continued in this slender silver form into the Peter Davison era.

The sonic screwdriver was often criticised by both viewers and the show's creative teams as being precisely the type of science fiction gimmick that *Doctor Who* should avoid – a universal problem solver which could

The sonic screwdriver first appeared in the 1968 adventure *Fury from the Deep*. Photo © BBC

be used to get the Doctor out of all sorts of scrapes. Consequently, there were several moves away from its use as an excuse to easily get the Doctor out of trouble. Unfortunately this did not prevent that *other* universal problem solver, K9, from being able to blast locks open on request! Eventually the programme's producer during the Eighties, John Nathan-Turner, decided that the Time Lord's special tools were getting him out of too many scrapes too easily and conveniently. Having despatched K9 into E-Space with the Doctor's other companion, the Time Lady Romana (who also had a sonic

Romana built her own in *The Horns of Nimon*. Photo © BBC

screwdriver of her own, which she built prior to *The Horns of Nimon*), the sonic screwdriver was finally written out in Part Three of Peter Davison's fourth transmitted story *The Visitation* in 1982. In that, the Doctor attempted to use it to free himself from the clutches of the Terileptil Leader. The alien then blasted it with his gun and destroyed the device, whereupon the Doctor commented: "I feel as if you've just killed an old friend!" The sonic screwdriver's final appearance was as a wrecked piece of metal in the fourth and last episode of the story, having outlasted many companions and for Doctors!

Andrew Pixley

Apart from its numerous uses as a device to unlock doors, manacles and other such things, the sonic screwdriver has been used for other things. Below is a short list of some of the more memorable uses:

Fury From the Deep: The Doctor opens an inspection hatch in the gas pipeline (first appearance).
The Dominators: Used like a laser cutting torch.
Inferno: Used by the Doctor and Liz Shaw as an electronic key into the garage where the TARDIS console was stored.
The Curse of Peladon: With a spinning mirror attached to its top, the Doctor hypnotises Aggedor, the Royal Beast of Peladon.
The Sea Devils: The Doctor uses it to find and detonate landmines and so scare off a Sea Devil.

The gadget conscious Third Doctor made frequent use of the device. Photo © BBC

The Three Doctors: The Doctor adjusts it to detect anti-matter in the Minsbridge Wildlife Sanctuary.
Carnival of Monsters: The screwdriver is used to detonate marsh gas and so keep the Drashigs away.
Death to the Daleks: Used to detect safe pathways through the Exxillon city.
Robot: Used to detonate landmines outside the Bunker and also cut

through the plated metal doorway.
The Sontaran Experiment: The Doctor repairs the transmat beacons with it. When Sarah finds the screwdriver abandoned, she knows the Doctor has been kidnapped.
Genesis of the Daleks: The screwdriver fails to work on Davros' office lock.
Terror of the Zygons: Used as a heat generator to set off the alarms in the Zygon spaceship.
The Face of Evil: The Doctor releases Leela from her trance.
The Invasion of Time: The sonic screwdriver fails to give the Doctor access to Borusa's private exit.
Destiny of the Daleks: The Doctor attempts to detonate a remote controlled bomb.
The Leisure Hive: The Doctor cuts his way out of the tachyon generator to stop himself being torn apart.
Four to Doomsday: The Doctor disables the manopticon machines with the screwdriver, and Nyssa disrupts one of the android bodies, with the help of a pencil.
Kinda: The screwdriver becomes an essential part of the delta wave augmentor that helps Nyssa to sleep soundly!

The Terileptil Leader responsible for the screwdriver's destruction. Photo © BBC

The Visitation: After attempting to escape his cell, the Doctor watches in horror as the Terileptil Leader destroys the sonic screwdriver with his laser gun.

In *Four to Doomsday*, Nyssa (Sarah Sutton) discovered a novel way of using the sonic screwdriver to defeat their enemies. Photo © BBC

Encounter on Burnt Snake Flat

She yelled and slammed on the brakes. She was right. It *was* him. As the red dust cloud drifted from round the Range Rover, his figure materialised out of the landscape. Squatting in the shade of a gum tree, abo-fashion, as if he was waiting for the Dreamtime to return.

He rose, pale coat pushed back, hands plunged into trouser pockets, and grinned boyishly as she almost fell out of the car.

"Doctor!"

"Tegan Jovanka." Her hand was shaken enthusiastically. "You got my note then."

"What note?"

"Ah." A frown. "Well, I expect you will . . . sometime."

"I can't believe it," she floundered. "I mean . . . what are you doing out here?"

He smiled and she went cold, easing back her hand. Why was he being nice to her? That exasperating reserve reeked of Englishness, even when he was an alien. What did he want? The sun was baking the back of her neck, but she'd frozen inside. "I mean it's not that I'm not glad to see you."

"No, of course not, Tegan."

"But to turn up . . . out of the blue."

"And what a blue." He gazed up into the depths overhead. "You should really wear a hat, you know. The ozone layer and all that."

"It's in the car," she heard herself saying.

There was a pause while his so innocent-looking blue eyes bored against her defensive mask. "You got back from London all right."

"You can see that, can't you?"

"And your family?"

"They had to wire me money. They still want to know where I'd been."

"Ah . . . But they're well?"

"Dad's laid up in hospital," she snapped. "So I'm running the farm."

"An accident, Tegan?"

"Sort of."

"What sort of 'sort of'?"

"What are you doing here?" she retaliated.

"Just a visit." He was needling his way back in. What did he know . . . suspect? Now he was walking off through the spinifex and she was following. "I've brought some things

you left behind. You left us rather suddenly."

"That was three years ago!"

"Really?" He sighed. "Well, I thought you might feel better by now. Less bitter?"

"Why?"

He turned, his patience evidently wearing thin. "Didn't you learn anything with me, Tegan? You must have got something out of it?"

She faltered and looked away.

"Tegan? I thought we were friends."

"I have fifteen hands working under me and a couple of thousand sheep. Why did you have to come back? It's so long ago, I sometimes wonder if you really existed – if it wasn't all a dream."

"A *bad* dream?"

"Sometimes. So many innocent people died. Sometimes it felt as if the world didn't have a future. I thought I was going mad!"

"So you shut it all out. Left it all behind."

"Did I?" She turned to fix him with a blazing stare, but he wasn't even looking at her. He was casting about for something along the edge of a half-dried pool.

"You came back to check up on me!" she accused.

"I am a Doctor, Tegan," he said, deep in his search. "So there's nothing to be afraid of."

"Nothing?"

He paused, squinting under a small rock with a satisfied smile. "What did you imagine?" He looked up at her again. "What did you say happened to your father?"

"None of your business!"

"Tegan!" The politeness had evaporated into a steely command.

She paused, her mouth drying up with fear. Avoiding his stare, she whispered, "It was a snakebite."

"Any snake in particular?"

"You know," she blurted. "You know which snake! The snake in my head."

"Like this?" he said.

She looked and saw the thing that he held in his hands, his fingers pinching the back of its head.

"No!"

"Is this what you think you've brought with you, Tegan?"

The reptile's dry skin shimmered as it coiled and writhed in his grasp.

"No! Take it away!"

"Is this what you've seen in your dreams?"

"Get it away from me!"

She was transfixed by the beady serpent stare as he brought it closer. The jaws opened and a diamond of venom hung on the curved needle fangs.

"What do you think it is, Tegan? Is this what's been coiling in the shadows of your mind all this time, waiting to strike again? It's a dark and evil thing, full of venom and hate. And you know its name, don't you?"

"No!"

Closer still it came and hissed its anger.

"Call it by its name, Tegan. Is it the Mara? Is that what you think?"

"No!" she cried. "It's not. It's just a snake."

With one movement, he flung the creature away from him across the pool that glittered with sunlight.

He held her gently for a long time. "Exactly. Just a snake," he said. "The Mara's long gone, I promised, remember?"

"How did you know?" she kept saying through her tears.

"I didn't until I called at the sheep station looking for you. The foreman says your father will be fine."

He glanced at the small brown waterhole. "Is that what they call a billabong?"

She half-grinned at last. "You never change, do you, Doctor? Always expecting the worst."

"You too, Tegan."

She sniffed and completed the grin. "Your celery needs changing," she said.

Marc Platt

TERRIBLE TUNES

‹Fade out Music›

All right pop pickers, this is formidable **WHO FM** here blasting through the airwaves with another incredible selection of tracks and wax. That was Bachman-Turner Overdrive with a Pop-tastic tune, *You aint seen nothing yet*, all right!

We slide on now with a top ten tunes inspired by that fabbo TV programme, *Doctor Who*, with the good Doc doing good all over the universe, just like all the work I do for charity that I don't like to talk about. Right!

Here we go then, hold on to your hats and let's rock!!!

Straight in at Number 10 it's the Timelords with *Doctorin' the TARDIS* mixing those mellow moody strains of Delia Derbyshire with the hard, fast,

glitter rock of my old mate Gazza Glitter.

At number 9, falling three places, we find the grand master himself, Jon Pertwee, with his lilting refrain *Who is the Doctor?* That's a re-issue chums.

Riding high at number 8, rising a Cliff-tastic two places, are The Earthlings with their rocky little *Landing of the Daleks*. One to smooch to there, girls!

Number 7 is where that bullish band of crazy Aussie rockers Bullamakanka are, with their classic track *Doctor Who is Gonna Fix It*. Rumour has it that Kylie Minogue will be covering this track on her next UK tour – you

heard it here first on fabulous **WHO FM!**

At number 6, rising twenty-seven places, Frazer Hines, current heart-throb of *Emmerdale* and erstwhile scottish companion with that top pop number *Who's Doctor Who?*

Falling to number 5 is the environmental concern record *Doctor . . . ?* by Blood Donor. Looks like they've run out of steam there.

And at number 4, for the third week, it's the diminutive starlet Roberta Tovey with the bouncy *Who's Who*.

Up to number 3 is a truly smashy piece of vinyl. From those cheeky

Slaves of Kane. It's *Abslom Daak - Dalek Killer* with more than a spoonful of The Stranglers thrown in.

At number 2, falling one place, is the top charity record *Doctor in Distress* sung by Who Cares. Right pop-pickers, buy it now and do your bit for charity!

And at number 1. For the first week. It's the Go Gos with their Daleky, Christmasy rendition of *I'm Gonna Spend my Christmas with a Dalek*. That's tinsel and more plum pudding for me. Oh yes!

That's all pop-pickers, and to see us out, another of my all-time fave raves. It's Bachman-Turner Overdrive, *'You aint seen nothing yet'* . . .

THE TOP TEN

1 **I Wanna Spend my Christmas with a Dalek**
2 **Doctor in Distress**
3 **Abslom Daak - Dalek Killer**
4 **Who's Who**
5 **Doctor . . . ?**
6 **Who's Dr Who?**
7 **Doctor Who is Gonna Fix It**
8 **Landing of the Daleks**
9 **Who is the Doctor?**
10 **Doctorin' the TARDIS**

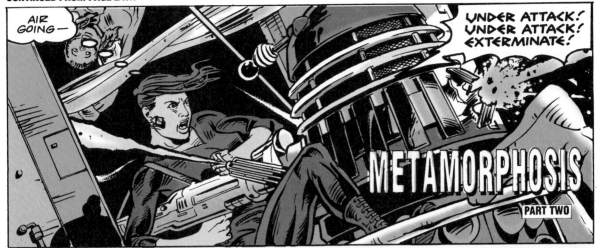

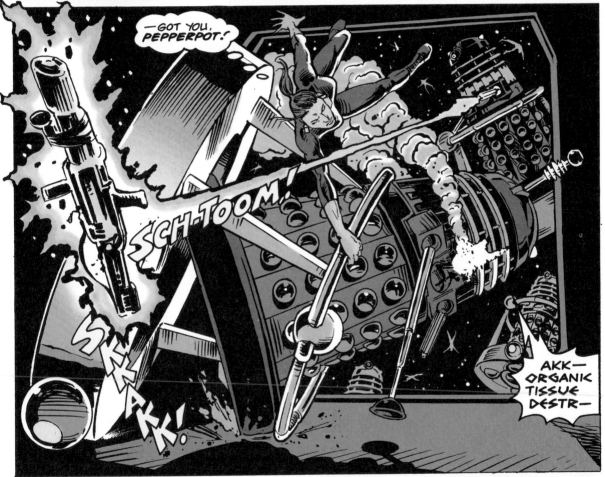

OUTER DOORS CLOSED, SEALS RESTORED. LIFE SUPPORT STABILISED—

PREPARE TO TRANSFER SURVIVING EMBRYOS TO DALEK SAUCER.

WAIT!

SCANNING SURVIVING HUMAN— ARCHIVE MATCH FOUND!

YOU ARE THE COMPANION OF THE DOCTOR! YOU WILL TAKE US TO HIM!

NO NEED, EITHER OF YOU...

I DECIDED TO COME TO YOU.

BACK IN THE MEDICAL LAB, MINUTES LATER—

—SO, THE DALEKS HAVE BEEN DIRECTING A MODULATED RADIATION BEAM AT THIS SHIP FROM THEIR OWN CRAFT, *MUTATING* THE EMBRYOS—AND ME AS WELL. THEY'RE TURNING THE EMBRYOS INTO *HUMAN/DALEK HYBRIDS.*

THAT'S *HORRIBLE!*

YES. BUT I BLOCKED THE SIGNAL WITH THE DISTRESS BEACON. SO THEY DECIDED TO TAKE MATTERS INTO THEIR OWN HANDS...

OR SUCKERS...

CORRECT...

THE MUTANTS WILL BE USED TO ADD A HUMAN FACTOR TO DALEK DESIGN—

WHAT, *AGAIN?!*

SILENCE. YOU ARE THE DOC-TOR, THE KA FARAQ GATRI.

YOU WILL STAY ON THE SHIP AFTER THE MUTATION BEAM HAS BEEN REACTIVATED.

ZZAP!

BRILLIANT! YES. TYPICAL DALEKS, ONE TRACK MINDS. THEY'RE SO OBSESSED WITH *ME* THEY DON'T EVEN THINK ABOUT ANYBODY ELSE.

IT'S A PITY THIS SHIP ISN'T ARMED...

DOCTOR! *THAT SMELL!*

YES, THEY'VE STARTED THE BEAM UP AGAIN. WE HAVEN'T VERY LONG —BUT THERE'S ONE CHANCE...

I KNOW YOU CAN HEAR ME... I'M *ONE* OF YOU... YOU MUST OBEY...

WICKED! HE'S CREATING SOME SORT OF TELEPATHIC LINK—

WE MUST... OBEY!

OBEY! OBEY! *OBEY!*

51

HE'S TURNING INTO A *DALEK!*

HE *ISN'T!* HE *CAN'T* BE!

OUTSIDE THE FREIGHTER...

DISABLED IN BATTLE. RETURNING TO SHIP.

SECURITY CODES CORRECT. PROCEED INSIDE SHIELDS.

OBEY... EGGS...

EGGS!

EXTERMINATE.!!

Dressing Up

As every *Doctor Who* fan knows, if you *really* want to get on, meet all the right people and make the most impact at conventions, you have to dress correctly.

Dress is vitally important to today's fan, as in the wild and wacky world of fandom you have to *be* somebody before you can get noticed. One only has to look at the Doctor to see how important dress and a sense of style is. Where would Troughton be without the rumpled jacket and baggy trousers? Similarly, Pertwee needs his velvet smoking jackets and ruffled shirts, while good old Tom cuts a dashing pose with his scarf, hat and overcoat.

Indeed, today's serious fan not only does his best to emulate his hero, but he uses only the very best items, collected over the years to the astonishment of his friends and family.

Here then, we present the definitive guide to *Doctor Who* dressing.

The fan must first and foremost have cultivated an unruly head of dark curly hair. This must be uncontrollable and will be seen poking out from anything he has on his head. Failing this, the Peter Davison 'bland' look can be adopted, with a thinning head of fine blonde hair.

On the head

The Dalek Hat: There are two versions of this, the first is quite old now (it was released in 1985), and if you can find one it has probably fallen apart at the seams. Of course the totally committed (and they should be) collector will have kept their hat in the freezer, thus minimising any damage. A better bet is the more recent hat, available from the MOMI exhibition in 1991. It still looks as silly as the original version, but costs about twice as much.

The Dalek Mask: Now these are very hard to find, but are well worth the effort. Basically resembling a papier mâché rubbish bin – similar to those you made at school during the art lessons – this incredible mask made you look and sound exactly like a Dalek (assuming that anyone thought a Dalek looked and sounded like a school-kid with a rubbish bin on his head).

Cyberman Mask: Not, as you may assume a full head mask, but a paper cut-out of a Cyberman that was held to the face with a piece of knicker elastic. This would only really fool your half-blind grannie, and even then she would have to see you face on. It was also too small. For the fan intent on one-upmanship, a better bet would be to track down the paper masks given away (you couldn't buy them) at the launch party for the MOMI exhibition. There were two designs, Dalek and Cyberman, both in an impressively garish colour scheme.

Doctor Who Caps: Not the sort that you could bang under your heel, but a horrible imported-from-America thing made from material and plastic. Sort of like a sun-visor for the Arctic Winter.

Tom Baker Mask: Now this is the ultimate. It came as part of a *Doctor Who* dressing up costume, and was as it sounds – a mask of Tom Baker. The mind boggles at the thought of hundreds of pint-sized Toms running around offering all and sundry jelly babies.

On the body

T-Shirts: Definitely a must. These days there are vast piles of T-shirts to choose from, ranging from the brilliant MOMI ones to the okay BBC Enterprises ones. The fan who wants to cut a dash will either have a personal one-off T-Shirt printed from an old piece of Lee Sullivan artwork (or Frank Bellamy if he is *really* posey) or will get Lee to draw a picture directly onto the T-Shirt. This is usually done using water-colours, thus meaning either a very smelly shirt, or Lee getting paid to do it again.

Tom Baker Costume: The other part of the costume that came with the mask. This was not so much a costume as a plastic T-shirt printed with the costume. Yes, a tartan waistcoat, jacket and scarf were printed onto a thin plastic shirt which only children of five or under could wear.

Doctor Who Outfit: Dapol to the rescue with some seventh Doctor cardigans, complete with question marks. What puzzles me is that the cardie is the one thing that people say they hate about the current costume – so why would they want to buy it?

Melanie Outfit: If the Seventh Doctor costume doesn't appeal, then perhaps a Melanie costume would. Somehow I can't see this at all.

Pyjamas: If it is real style you are after, then a pair of *Doctor Who* pyjamas are the thing for you. Again, only in sizes up to about a five-year-old, the pyjamas sold well for Mothercare.

On the bottom-half

Doctor Who Underpants: They had to get in somewhere. BHS's marvellous 1981 contribution to *Doctor Who* clothing is still a firm favourite with the ladies.

On the feet

Dalek Slippers: If flocking and corduroy are your thing, then perhaps you would go for these stylish and impressive foot coverings. Musician Mark Ayres well known for his *Who* compositions, swears by them.

Doctor Who Slippers: Released with the pyjamas, these matching slippers are fetchingly finished with special non-slip soles. A must for the house, bedroom or bonfire.

On the hands

Gloves: Yet again made only for people with very small hands, the gloves were emblazoned with the *Doctor Who* logo. The problem with them was that no air could circulate (like, for example, rubber washing up gloves) and water had an annoying habit of dripping from the fingers whenever the glove was compressed. This gives new meaning to the phrase, a damp handshake.

In the pockets

Just about *anything* really, but the considered fan will limit the items to those really relevant to his mission in life. Obvious essentials are a bag of jelly babies – the superior fan can substitute licorice allsorts (as long as he can explain *why!*), or a junior-size bottle of gin, a sonic screwdriver (imported from America at ludicrous cost), a yo-yo, a batmobile model, a 'zoids' model, an old fashioned recorder, a diary with '500 years' written on the cover in crayon, a cricket ball, a set of Paul Daniels' magic tricks, two spoons and an old-fashioned watch with case.

David J Howe

BRIEF ENCOUNTER

A TOURIST INVASION

The Oox (translated in their language as "those who communicate in a decent low pitched modulation") did not like the Iix. (Iix was a word in the Oox language meaning "those who communicate in a very unpleasant high-pitched, squeaky and thoroughly obnoxious way").

Not unsurprisingly the latter referred to themselves in their language as "delightfully light-toned superior ones" – the "Khee"; the self-styled "Oox" were the "Khoogh" ("gratingly heavy-toned eaters of daarg-droppings"). The Khee were more than a little hypocritical in this reference to their enemies, as they would have been more than happy to consume daarg-droppings themselves, if they had had the opportunity. Unfortunately, for them, daargs were only to be found in the land of the Oox. Daarg droppings were a much coveted delicacy. In

fact, the only species that could resist daarg-droppings were the daargs themselves, who couldn't understand what all the fuss was about but much appreciated the double advantage of being offered copious supplies of food by all and sundry and not having to worry about waste-disposal.

Occasionally, an unusually enlightened Khee or Oox would attain brief prominence and argue that, from the minor difference in the pitch of their voices, there were no discernible differences between their races. Indeed a gathering of mute Oox and Khee would have no means of distinguishing one from another. But the idea of any rapprochement always fell on deaf, or rather too highly tuned, ears.

Over many generations of border disputes, skirmishes and minor wars both races had survived in a state of fluctuating parity. But that was all about to change. The Khee had

invented the Megahurts – a biotechnical "loudspeaker" of gargantuan size that was designed to resonate at a frequency fatal to Oox sense and sensibility. The Khee were in the process of trundling this massive structure slowly towards the Oox borders where it would be capable of causing maximum damage to their foe.

Meanwhile, the Oox were deploying their newly invented nerve gas which would react only on the Khee voice box, cause it to expand rapidly and prevent them from breathing.

The Doctor and Mel had been on Tribolyca for only a brief time but it had seemed much longer. The Tribolycanna were obsessively hospitable and terminally garrulous. It was universally acknowledged that before enquiring as to a Tribolycan's health, you should ensure that you had a packed lunch. In fact, such questions were best avoided altogether. However, the Doctor had felt constrained to come to their aid when he had discovered that their genetic inability to refuse hospitality was being abused by an Earth based travel agency offering very competitive, cheap holidays for the deaf and hard of hearing (on the very sensible basis that any other group would subsequently sue for damages for boredom).

Selachos Bdella Travel Inc. were able to do this and realised a massive profit as their only cost was the travel to Tribolyca; all accommodation and food being provided free by the Tribolycanna. But as theirs was not a planet rich in either mineral resources or food supply, the Doctor felt that a limited intervention to protect them from exploitation and ultimate extinction was not unjustifiable.

At first, the Doctor attempted to persuade the Tribolycanna to solve their own problem by refusing hospitality to the tourists. Their reply (abbreviated for the reader's benefit from its original three hour length) was to the effect that even though they were aware that they were being comprehensively robbed, they were no more capable of denying hospitality to a traveller than were the inhabitants of Chaite of having a haircut. Never having heard of Chaite or its hirsute (or bald?) inhabitants, the Doctor longed to enquire further but forbore out of consideration for Mel, who was becoming visibly impatient. (A human's short life span makes them incapable of enjoying a really good conversation).

The Doctor had eventually solved the problem, rather neatly in his opinion, by immersing a slow-release sulphur "bomb" in the network of warm springs on Tribolyca, which caused the immediate departure of the tourists and subsequent bankrupting of Selachos Bdella Travel Inc. The Tribolycanna, mercifully, had no sense of smell and were only aware that their geysers were now of a different and most pleasant hue.

As the TARDIS door swung shut behind them, abruptly cutting off the continuing and insistent chorus of gratitude from the Tribolycanna, Mel took a deep breath of comparatively fresh air and stared accusingly at the Doctor.

"I don't suppose it occurred to you to warn me that you were intending to create the biggest stink-bomb in the Universe! I didn't know whether to stick my fingers in my ears for relief from their incessant droning or to hold my nose! What's next?... a guided tour of a volcano, tea with Torquemada?"

"No, he makes a terrible cup of tea. Never warms the pot," grinned the Doctor. "I've been thinking for a long time that we deserve a little treat. I know just the place," he added as he launched himself at the TARDIS console.

And so it was that they found themselves standing on a small green island in the middle of a vast expanse of blue sea gazing at a sky filled with a myriad of interconnecting and pulsating rainbows which revolved around a vortex of such incandesent beauty that Mel could only gasp with wonder.

After standing in blissful silence for a long time, Mel turned to the Doctor and slowly asked "Not the Eye of Orion?... At last!"

He nodded down at her indulgently with only a trace of a triumphant smirk.

After the Tardis had left its vantage point some hours later, the travellers were unaware that where it had stood were the crushed and obliterated remains of the entire civilisations of the Oox and the Khee, their armies, their cities and their people.
Colin Baker

Monster File
The DRACONIANS

Frontier in Space Photograph © BBC - Art © Steve Dillon

NAME:
The Draconians

PLANET OF ORIGIN: Draconia

KNOWN ALLIES:
The Doctor; Humans

KNOWN ENEMIES:
The Master; Daleks

BASE OF OPERATIONS:
Draconia

FIRST APPEARANCE:
Frontier in Space

The Empire of Draconia is home to one of the galaxy's proudest, most intelligent races mankind has ever encountered.

At one point, however, both the Draconian Empire and the Earth Federation were at war, with terrible casualties on both sides. After much negotiation, an uneasy peace was declared, with both parties setting up a frontier on the edges of their respective agreed spatial zones.

This treaty was almost broken when the Daleks, via their agent the Master, tried to provoke a second war, enabling them to conquer both sides of the frontier.

Disaster was averted due to the Doctor's intervention, and both races learned to live together in peace. By joining forces to defeat the Daleks it was soon all too obvious that an alliance was the only way forward for two such great powers.

Monster File
SILURIANS
and the SEA DEVILS

The Sea Devils Photograph © BBC - Silurian Art © David Lloyd

NAME: The Silurians and Sea Devils

PLANET OF ORIGIN: Earth

KNOWN ALLIES: The Master

KNOWN ENEMIES: The Doctor; UNIT; The Royal Navy

BASE OF OPERATIONS: Underground and underwater

FIRST APPEARANCE: *The Silurians/The Sea Devils*

The Silurians were first discovered living in underground chambers in Derbyshire, near the site of a top secret scientific complex. A reptilian race, it has been suggested they should more accurately be termed the Eocenes, because that is the prehistoric stage of Earth's development from which they came. The creatures fled to their underground bunkers and into a state of hibernation to avoid destruction, when an approaching planetoid threatened to devastate the planet. The planetoid in fact became Earth's moon and the Silurians never came out of their hibernation.

The Sea Devils were aquatic cousins to the Silurians, but both groups formed an alliance during the late Twenty-First Century, to try and provoke a war between differing political human factions; they would then have reclaimed what they consider *their* world once and for all...

Monster File
The OGRONS

Frontier in Space Photograph © BBC – Art © Lee Sullivan

NAME: The Ogrons

PLANET OF ORIGIN: An unnamed planet

KNOWN ALLIES: The Daleks; The Master

KNOWN ENEMIES: The Doctor; UNIT; Draconians; Amorphous monster on their home planet

BASE OF OPERATIONS: Mobile

FIRST APPEARANCE: *Day of the Daleks*

The Ogrons are a simian race of mercenaries possessing limited intelligence but a fierce loyalty to whoever employs them.

The planet they come from is on the outer rim of the galaxy, beyond the borders of Earth's Federation and the Draconian Empire's frontiers. It is a desolate, harsh world, and the Ogrons both worship and live in dread of a huge carnivorous creature that lives there.

The Daleks have been known to employ the Ogrons twice in their attempted conquests, first in Earth's Twenty-Second century and later in the Twenty-Sixth. There, alongside the Master, the Daleks used them in an attempt to provoke a second galactic war between Earth and Draconia.

The Ogrons were once described as being like guard dogs, loyal but incapable of acting on their own initiative. They remain, however, a strong and frightening force in their own right...

Monster File
The DÆMONS

The Dæmons Photograph © BBC - Art © David Lloyd

NAME: The Dæmons

PLANET OF ORIGIN: Damos

KNOWN ALLIES: (Originally) The Master

KNOWN ENEMIES: The Doctor; UNIT; The Master

BASE OF OPERATIONS: Devil's End, England

FIRST APPEARANCE: The Dæmons

Although resembling the traditional Devil of English folklore, the Dæmons are actually an ancient race of powerful aliens who set up a series of scientific experiments throughout the cosmos.

One of these experiments was in fact on the planet Earth and when the Master, using the ancient psionic energy to awaken the slumbering Dæmon Azal, showed the Dæmon what the Earth was like, Azal decided the experiment was a failure.

However, destroying the Earth would be wasteful of what little energy he had so Azal agreed to hand over control to the Master, until the Doctor's intervention. The Doctor begged Azal to leave the humans to better themselves and although Azal realised that Earth had potential, the illogical emotions of the Doctor's assistant Jo Grant caused him to accidentally destroy himself via the same psionic power that he normally thrived upon...

Frontier in Space Photograph © BBC - Art © Steve Dillon